Introduction to Podcast Technology

DISCOVER THE ESSENTIAL TOOLS AND
TECHNIQUES YOU NEED TO RECORD,
PRODUCE AND LAUNCH YOUR PODCAST

DAVID POWER

POWER MEDIA GROUP
BROOKLYN, NEW YORK

David Power/ Power Media Group
Brooklyn, NY
davidpower.com

Book Layout ©2013 BookDesignTemplates.com

Introduction to Podcast Technology
David Power – 1st ed.
ISBN: 978-1535229890

PODCAST TECHNOLOGY DEMYSTIFIED

SINCE YOU'VE OPENED this book and are curious enough to read these first few sentences, there's a good chance you're interested in podcasting but you may feel confused, intimidated, or overwhelmed by the technology.

There's good news... You're not alone!

As an experienced podcaster and podcasting coach and instructor, I've found that people fail during their first attempt at podcasting for a very limited number of reasons:

1. They hold the belief that *"I'm not a technical person"* and as soon as they discover podcasting requires technical skills, they feel intimidated, drop the idea and never get started.

2. They're **uninformed about the hardware and software** required to create high-quality recordings. Because of misinformation, some people buy too much gear and get overwhelmed by either the expense or the complexity of making it all work together. Others buy too little or the wrong type of gear only to discover their recordings sound terrible. In both cases, these people often get frustrated and give up before they launch their first episode.

3. They **underestimate the time it takes** to record, edit, mix, process, master, encode, tag and upload each podcast episode. They get one or two episodes under their belt, realize it requires a much greater time

commitment than they're able to manage and they give up.

If you're in one of these categories, this book will help you overcome the beliefs, assumptions and misinformation that have prevented your success in the past.

If you're brand new to podcasting and have found this book before face-planting into one of these hurdles, that's wonderful. I'm certain this book will prevent you from wasting a lot of time, energy and money by demystifying the tools and techniques you need in order to be successful.

LET'S BE CLEAR

Before we go any further, I want us to be clear on one very important truth. A truth that is absolutely crucial to your success as a podcaster. It's so important that it should be emphasized. Here it is:

*Technology is **not** the most important aspect of podcasting.*

It may seem odd for a book on podcast technology to admit (and emphasize) this fact. But I believe honesty is always the best policy, so let me explain further.

Think of podcasting as an art form. It's not much of a stretch. Podcasts are often informative, entertaining, thought-provoking and sometimes even disturbing – in much the same way a painting, poem, stage play, piece of music or film (all art forms in their own right) can create an emotional response.

Almost every creative pursuit requires tools. For a painter, it's the canvas, brush and paint. For a sculptor, it's the hammer, chisel and stone. For a musician, it's the cello, piano or guitar. And for a filmmaker, it's the camera, lights, script and actors.

Successful artists know it's almost impossible to master their art form until they master the tools used to create the art. It just so happens that the tools in the art of podcasting are high-tech tools. They include microphones, recorders, interfaces, software, plugins, hosting services and distribution networks. And while it may not be necessary to truly master each and every one of these tools, it's absolutely crucial that you're aware of and competent with most of them.

The goal of this book is not to turn you into a master recording engineer. No single book – no matter how well-written – can accomplish that. Instead, my intention is to focus on the fundamental building blocks of podcast technology – topics that, in my experience, have been the biggest obstacles for beginning podcasters.

This book has been designed to help you build a solid foundation of knowledge, a curiosity to learn more and to develop a practice in using the tools we're going to discuss.

Here's just some of what you'll learn from this book:

- How to tell the difference between a good recording room and a bad one. (*And how to avoid wasting time and money when improving a bad room.*)

- Learn the two main types of microphones and why only one of them is appropriate for most podcasters.

- Discover the difference between an *audio interface* and an *audio recorder*. (*And which to choose if you can only afford one or the other.*)

- Discover the one recording accessory that can make the biggest improvement in the quality of your recordings. (*You'll be surprised how inexpensive this one is.*)

- How to configure free software (*used by a lot of podcasting pros*) to convert master recordings to MP3.

- Learn what to look for (*and look out for*) when choosing a media host.

- Discover the most effective method to get your show listed in the *iTunes* podcast directory.

What this book **won't cover** includes:

- The science of sound (or the science of *anything*) – To be transparent, I'm a scientist at heart. If pushed, I can talk for days about physics, electronics and software development. But instead of spending valuable time reviewing a lot of theory, we're going focus on how to apply modern tools and techniques to creating a podcast. In other words, we'll focus on information you need, not on information you don't need.

- The history of podcasting – No matter what you consider to be its official birth date, podcasting is less than 20 years old. If you're reading this book, there's a good chance podcasting started in your lifetime. It's not that interesting things haven't happened during that period – but with such a limited history, facts, figures, names and faces are not difficult to find. We don't need to spend time recapping them in this book.

- How easy it is to podcast – I'll avoid going on a rant here but any who tells you *podcasting is easy* isn't being completely honest. First of all, the term 'easy' is relative. It's *relatively* easy for NBA star LeBron James to sink a three-point basket. It's not easy for me. Unlike many books on podcasting, this one won't try to convince you all the technical stuff is simple and then leave you to figure out all the buttons, dials and cables on your own. Instead, this book walks you through the podcast creation process step by step from beginning to end. Easy? No. But, doable? Abso-freakin-lutely!

I admit that some concepts and techniques we'll cover in this book are difficult to convey using only the written word. That's an unfortunate limitation of books for instructing on complex and technical topics.

To address this limitation, I've created the **Introduction to Podcast Technology** online course as a companion to this book. As a collection of voice, text, moving and still images presented in video format, the course makes it a lot easier to demonstrate some of the more complex techniques discussed in the book. Best of all, as an owner of this book, the course is completely free to you.

*Enroll in the **Introduction to Podcast Technology** video course for free. Visit the following link for details:*

http://podcasttechnologycourse.com/intro

HOW TO USE THIS BOOK

CHANCES ARE this isn't the first book you've read, so I think I'm safe in assuming you don't need a lot of instruction on how books are used.

However, having spent a lot of time writing and organizing the material in this book, I have four recommendations:

1. **Read the book from beginning to end in the order it's presented.** Chapters are organized in a logical order that follows the podcast creation process. For instance, you can't upload your MP3 file until you've recorded your episode. And you can't record an episode until you've plugged in your microphone. For the most part, chapters also build in complexity. Reading chapters in order will ensure you don't encounter terms or techniques that are unclear or confusing because they were covered in an earlier chapter you haven't yet read.

2. **Complete the assignments at the end of each chapter.** Reading this book will provide you with a solid understanding of podcast technology. Actively participating in the assignments will strengthen your understanding greatly. We all learn and retain more information by *doing* than we do by solely *reading*. It may not be possible for you to complete all the assignments on your first pass through the book. That's okay. Do your best to complete as many assignments as possible on your first pass and return later to finish the rest.

3. **Return to the book and re-read chapters that interest you and/or topics you didn't completely understand the first time through.** Some topics will interest you more than others. If you'd like to re-read a chapter purely for enjoyment, I highly encourage that. On the other hand, if you didn't completely grasp a topic on your first pass through the book, a second read (and a second stab at the chapter assignment) might be just what you need to solidify your understanding.

4. **Enroll in the free *Introduction to Podcast Technology* video course.** I think you'll find this book covers key podcast technology topics in a complete and thorough fashion. However, there are some tools and techniques that are difficult to teach through only words on a page. To address this, I've created an online video course that lets you look over my shoulder as I demonstrate: a) how to apply equalization filters to your recorded audio; b) how to convert a WAV file to an MP3; and c) how to submit your podcast to the *iTunes* directory. These are just three examples. The course has a dedicated module for each chapter in this book – plus some other goodies I think you'll enjoy! Watching me perform complex editing and processing techniques on a computer screen will take your understanding to an entirely new level. The best part? As an owner of the **Introduction to Podcast Technology** book, enrollment in this online course is

available to you ***absolutely free***. If you haven't already enrolled, here's the link once again:

http://podcasttechnologycourse.com/intro

I hope you enjoy reading this book. More importantly, I hope it removes any technology overwhelm or intimidation you might be feeling and inspires you to create a podcast and deliver it to the world.

If you have questions you'd like answered or feedback you'd like to share, you can contact me through the following link:

http://masterpodcaster.com/podcasttech

Best of luck,

David Power
Brooklyn, New York – July 2016

Contents

FREE VIDEO COURSE

THANK YOU!

As a sincere thank you for reading this book, I'm
offering you complimentary enrollment in my
Introduction to Podcast Technology video course.
Follow the link below for FREE instant access:

http://podcasttechnologycourse.com/intro

[1]

Room Acoustics

O N THE SURFACE, it might seem that the subject of *room acoustics* isn't exactly a technology topic. But trust me, it truly is. The science of sound is far more complex than most of the topics we'll cover in this book. In fact, there are laboratories full of people with advanced degrees (and white lab coats) all around the world studying the science of sound.

We won't get into a lot of the technical details of acoustics in this chapter, or anywhere else in this book. Instead, we'll focus on the practical aspects and answer two important questions:

1. What makes a room sound good or bad?

2. How can we create a good recording in a bad room?

If you're not yet convinced of the importance of room acoustics, let me relate a personal experience.

A few years ago, I bought a book titled *Mixing Secrets for the Small Studio* by Mike Senior. Mike is a well-known and successful recording engineer and the book is a great one to read if you want to get more into the nuts-and-bolts of studio recording. If you're interested in this book, here's a link:

> **Mixing Secrets for the Small Studio by Mike Senior:**
>
> *http://masterpodcaster.com/mixingsecrets*

Being an audio geek at heart, I was excited to dig into this book. So, on the New York City subway one morning, I cracked it open (as much as you can *crack* a Kindle without breaking it) and started reading.

I wanted Mike to jump right into telling me what dials to turn and what buttons to push. By the end of my morning commute, I expected to know exactly how to make my podcast recordings sound like they were produced in a million-dollar studio.

But instead of diving into the sexy stuff, the book opened with a very detailed, very technical discussion of room acoustics and monitoring. I was hugely disappointed.

I'd bought this book to learn about knobs and buttons and faders. Not room acoustics and waterfall charts. But Mike Senior convinced me (very slowly, mind you) how important room acoustics are. He also made it clear that most home studios ignore acoustics. And that's why most home studio recordings sound like... well... home studio recordings.

I knew my studio (which is actually a small office in my home) sounded terrible. But I didn't understand why until I read this book.

As disappointed as I was with the first section of *Mixing Secrets*, Mike eventually won me over. And that led to me spending more money than I want to admit treating my room with professional acoustic panels. The room still isn't perfect. But it's infinitely better. It's now squarely in the *acceptable* category.

THE BASICS OF ACOUSTICS

I promised we wouldn't spend too much time on the science behind room acoustics. It can be dry and tedious.

All you really need to understand is that when you make a sound in any room – by speaking, plucking a guitar string, hitting a drum, etc. – sound waves travel outward from the source in all directions much like ripples when you throw a stone into a pond.

Except – unlike pond ripples – sound waves move in three dimensions: outward towards the walls, but also towards the ceiling and floor. These sound waves then reflect off of these surfaces and continue to bounce around the room until they run out of energy and die.

However, while they're bouncing around the room, sound waves interfere with one another in mysterious ways that depend on the dimensions of the room, the amount of furniture it contains, what the furniture is made of, and the position of your ears and/or microphone. To make things more complicated, different sound frequencies react and interfere in different ways – sometimes sounding louder, sometimes quieter. Almost never *better*.

The bottom line is that all these bounces and interferences can sound terrible when your microphone picks them up and records them to your hard drive or memory card.

CHARACTERISTICS OF A BAD ROOM

A *bad room* is one that displays one or more the following acoustic characteristics when a sound is produced:

1. Echo, slap-back or reverberation. These terms describe different types of sound reflections. You're likely familiar with the term *echo*. *Slap-back* is very similar and often used interchangeably with *echo*. *Reverberation* refers to a series of reflections that blur together to create a slowly-decaying trail of sound after the original sound is produced. All of these phenomena can negatively impact the intelligibility and perceived quality of a podcast recording.

2. Higher sound volume in the corners of the room than in the center.

3. *Nulling* (or decrease in volume) of certain frequencies depending on your listening position.

Bad rooms can display other symptoms but these are the big three. And for podcasting, it's the first group (echo, slap-back or reverberation) that is of particular concern.

If you listen to podcasts regularly (You do, right?), you've noticed some shows sound like they were recorded in a submarine (in other words, *terrible*). And others sound like they were engineered by Mike Senior himself.

I'm not going to attempt to convince you to spend thousands of dollars treating your room with expensive acoustic paneling. If you've got the budget, by all means go for it. You won't be disappointed.

But a dedicated, acoustically-treated room is not an absolute necessity. You can achieve perfectly-acceptable results as long as you have a basic awareness of what makes a room sound bad and are willing to spend a little time and effort making good choices regarding your recording environment and the gear you use.

If you Google "DIY studio acoustics", you'll get thousands of search results. And each of those results will propose a different solution on how to turn your room into a professional-sounding studio. Unfortunately, many of those "solutions" are worthless.

I've experimented with a lot of these DIY suggestions over time and compiled a list of those that just don't work. So save your time, money and sanity and just skip them. Here's the list:

"Solutions" That Just Don't Work

Bookshelves

Books and the shelves they sit on have hard surfaces so they tend to reflect sounds much in the same way a wall or ceiling does. If there happen to be bookshelves in your recording room, there's no need to remove them. Just don't expect them to make a positive difference.

MOVING BLANKETS

Moving blankets are soft and thin. They cut a little of the higher frequencies but almost none of the lower frequencies. And the *low end* is where 95% of your room's problems are. Don't waste your time on blankets.

EGG CRATES AND FOAM PADS

These materials are similar in construction to moving blankets. They're soft and thin and cut only higher frequencies. I suggest skipping them.

MATTRESSES

Really? Who has enough mattresses to cover the walls and ceiling of a room? Not to mention, mattresses are a lot more expensive than professional acoustic panels. And please, DO NOT tell me you pulled eight mattresses off the sidewalk in your neighborhood and lined your walls with them. Because. That's. Just. Gross.

RECORDING IN A CLOSET

This one *might* work. But, whether it works or not depends more on the size, dimensions and layout of the room than it does on the fact it contains clothing on hangers. Clothing is a lot like moving blankets – thin and soft. You can always give your closet a try. If it sounds good, it may be an option for you. But closets typically aren't convenient for setting up recording gear, or inviting guests in for interviews. Your mileage may vary.

MICROPHONE SHIELDS

These devices are known by several different names but they generally look like the image found at the following link.

Microphone Shield:

http://masterpodcaster.com/micshield

The theory behind a microphone shield is scientifically sound. They're designed to absorb and reduce the energy in your voice before it bounces off a wall and returns to the microphone as a reflection. The problem with microphone shields is they're generally too small to make a difference. In a 10' x 10' room, you'll typically be dealing with at least 520 square feet of wall, ceiling and floor area. The typical microphone shield offers only between three to six square feet of acoustic absorption. That amounts to approximately 1% of the reflective surfaces in the room – generally not enough surface area to make a noticeable difference.

MORE EXPENSIVE MICROPHONES

This is one of the most misguided and ridiculous DIY solutions ever suggested. If a *microphone* sounds bad because it's cheap, that's a problem you can solve by purchasing a better microphone.

But if a *room* sounds bad to a cheap microphone, it's going to sound bad to an expensive microphone. Perhaps even worse. DO NOT believe anyone who tells you room acoustics issues can be solved by spending more money on gear. They don't know what they're talking about.

With that said, there is one type of microphone that can improve the quality of your recordings in a bad room. And it's not necessarily more expensive, just different. We'll talk more about that in the next chapter.

THREE WAYS TO IMPROVE YOUR RECORDINGS

So, if you have a room that doesn't sound great, what can you do to improve it? I'm glad you asked. Here are a few suggestions.

INSTALL PROFESSIONAL ROOM TREATMENT

As I mentioned earlier, this isn't a cheap option. If you purchase the right quantity of acoustic panels (often known as *bass traps*) and install them in the right places, you can turn a bad room into a good one. Almost like magic. But because of the cost involved, this is not a solution I recommend to anyone who's just starting out in podcasting. Later maybe, but not yet.

RECORD IN YOUR CAR

Yes. You read that correctly. The interior of the average motor vehicle makes a great vocal recording booth.

Think about it. Cars have:

- Irregular shapes: Seats, dashboards, headrests, etc.

- No parallel surfaces: Slanted windows

- A lot of soft, dense materials: Carpeted floors, upholstered seats and roof interior

I've listened to a podcast recorded by the host in the back seat of his wife's Toyota Prius. And it sounded fantastic.

Now I'll admit, it's not always (or ever) convenient to record a podcast inside a car. But it's good to know it can produce quality results if you ever find yourself in a pinch.

Okay, there's one more solution that works well. And it's probably the best and quickest way to make a big impact.

USE THE RIGHT TYPE OF MICROPHONE

I hinted at this earlier. And no, it doesn't necessarily mean spending more money. In fact, you *might* need to spend less money. More on that in the next chapter.

ASSIGNMENT #1

FIND YOUR PODCAST RECORDING ROOM

Before you move on to the next chapter, walk through your house, apartment, basement or other available space and listen very closely.

Rooms close to sources of noise (i.e. a furnace or air conditioner, a window facing a busy street, etc.) aren't good choices. Same goes for rooms with bad acoustics. Clap your hands in each room and listen. Can you hear the echo of the clap for a second after your hands meet? If so, it's not a good choice. Keep searching until you identify the quietest and best-sounding room available to you. And then stake your claim to it. This will be *your* Podcasting Room.

[2]

Microphones

IN **THIS CHAPTER**, we dive head first into one of my favorite topics.

When it comes to podcasting, microphones are super-important. Choosing the right one for the job is important, mounting it correctly is important, and applying the proper technique is important.

In fact, it's not a stretch to say that without a microphone, there can be no podcast. You need a link between your voice and your recording device and the microphone is that link.

There are two main types of microphones used in podcasting:

1. *condenser* microphones; and

2. *dynamic* microphones

Let's discuss each type in greater detail.

CONDENSER MICROPHONES

Condenser microphones are generally more sensitive than dynamic microphones. This can be both a blessing and a curse.

On the *blessing* side, a high-quality condenser picks up all the nuances in your voice – the highs, the lows and everything in between. Even the quietest whispers retain all their detail.

On the *curse* side (if I can be dramatic for a moment), a condenser microphone also picks up a lot of sounds you don't want your podcast audience to hear. For example:

- It can hear the fan in your computer

- And every key press on your computer keyboard

- And the TV upstairs

- And traffic in the street

- And the guy mowing his lawn four houses away

You get the picture.

Condenser microphones hear *almost everything*. And that means *almost everything* ends up in your podcast recording. And that's not what you want.

If it sounds like I'm condemning condenser microphones, I'm not. In a good recording environment, a condenser microphone may be exactly what you want. This is why condensers are used in professional studios for close to 80 percent of all vocal recordings.

When a room is quiet and has proper acoustic treatment, a high-quality condenser microphone can sound spectacular.

But in a less-than-perfect room – that is, the type of room most podcasters record in – a condenser is not always the best choice.

What does that leave you?

DYNAMIC MICROPHONES

Dynamic microphones – particularly those designed for broadcasting – are less sensitive to noises that aren't directly in front of them.

This means if your mouth is two to four inches away from a dynamic microphone, it will hear you loud and clear.

But the sounds you don't want – things like your computer, air conditioner, television and street noise – those sounds don't make it onto your recording. Or, if the microphone does pick them up, they're typically at such low levels they're generally not noticeable. Based on this description, you might get the impression that a dynamic microphone is always the best choice. This isn't necessarily the case.

It's simply that dynamic and condenser microphones are different tools for different jobs and different environments. And it just so happens that dynamic microphones are generally excellent tools for podcasters.

And what dynamic microphones do I recommend to podcasters?

My answer will depend on your budget.

PROFESSIONAL OPTIONS

If you can afford to spend several hundred dollars, I'd recommend one of the following dynamic microphones:

- Heil Sound PR 40

- Shure SM7B

The SM7B is a microphone I personally own and it's always produced excellent results. One of its claims-to-fame is that Michael Jackson used this microphone for all the vocal recordings on the *Thriller* album (the best-selling album of all time.) And Michael could afford to use any microphone on the planet. I acknowledge, Michael wasn't known for podcasting. But still.

Both the PR 40 and the SM7B microphones are used in radio stations around the world. In recent years, they've also become very popular among podcasters who have a few dollars to spend. If you can afford one of these, you won't be disappointed. You can get excellent results with either of them.

Once you've gotten some experience under your belt and you're certain podcasting is something you want to do for the long term, it might make sense to invest in one or both of these microphones and accessories for them.

But if you're just starting out and don't have the budget for these professional microphones, what can you do?

BUDGET OPTIONS

I'm happy to say there are a couple of really good budget options available. And I think you'll be surprised by how affordable they are.

The first is the *Shure SM58*. If you've ever seen a live band perform – either in a nightclub or stadium – there's a good chance every singer on the stage was using an SM58. It's the most commonly-used stage vocal microphone in the world. And for two very important reasons:

1. *It's built like a tank.* The Shure company website has a video of an SM58 being repeatedly dropped onto pavement from a helicopter, then plugged in and used to record the video narrator's voice. For all intents and purposes, it's indestructible.

2. *It has great rear rejection.* This means it hears only the sounds immediately in front of the diaphragm and not those behind or to the sides of it. This is important in amplified live shows where ear-splitting feedback can be a painful problem.

The SM58 hovers around USD $100 and with the proper accessories, it can produce great podcast recordings.

All three microphones we've discussed so far have balanced, XLR outputs. This means they need a preamplifier to boost the signal to a level that can be recorded.

> **Note:** *XLR refers to a three-conductor cable and connector used in professional recording gear. It's designed and constructed to minimize noise levels.*

What's that? You can't afford a preamplifier right now? Luckily, there's another option worth considering. It's the *Audio-Technica ATR2100*. This is a sub-$100 microphone with both USB and professional XLR outputs.

I'm going to be brutally honest with you. For the longest time I was dead set against USB microphones. Because they were inexpensive, I assumed they produced low-quality recordings.

I held this belief until I heard one being used by an experienced podcaster. And it sounded amazing – on par with much more expensive microphones.

So I rushed out and bought one (or more correctly, had one rush-delivered to me) so I could hear it with my own ears.

If you visit the link below, you'll hear a side-by-side comparison between my ATR2100 and my Shure SM7B.

ATR2100 vs. SM7B:

http://masterpodcaster.com/atr2100vssm7b

If your ears are well-trained and you listen very closely, you'll notice some differences between these microphones. I can hear these differences myself when I listen to side-by-side recordings through good speakers. But the differences are very, very small.

It's worth mentioning, because the ATR2100 is a USB microphone, it doesn't require a preamp or interface. You can plug it directly into your computer and start recording right away. This means a new podcaster with a small budget can get up and running for a very small investment.

Let me be clear, I'm not beating up on expensive gear. Expensive gear definitely has its place. I own a lot of it myself. The message I want to deliver is that when you're starting out in podcasting, you should buy the best gear you can comfortably afford and focus on learning to use it properly.

If your budget is $1,000, you can build yourself a really great kit. But if your budget is only $100, you can still get a microphone and a couple of key accessories and start recording your podcast pretty much immediately.

With USB microphones like the ATR2100 available on Amazon.com – and shipped to your door within two days – price is no longer an obstacle to creating a high-quality podcast.

To recap, the ATR2100 is a dynamic microphone that's great for less-than-perfect recording rooms. It requires no preamp and it comes with all the cables you need to hook it up. It even has the ability to connect to a microphone preamp if that's something you want to do in the future. If your budget is tight, it's hard to go wrong with the ATR2100.

ASSIGNMENT #2

GET YOURSELF A MICROPHONE

Armed with the information in this chapter, you're now an educated microphone shopper.

By all means, feel free to do more research. Find some in-depth reviews, opinions and side-by-side comparisons online. More information is always better than less. But don't research forever. That's a mistake I've made far too often.

Narrow down your microphone options to one or two models within your budget and make it happen.

Bring that microphone home (or have it delivered) and get prepared for the next chapter.

[3]

Audio Interfaces and Recorders

IN THE LAST CHAPTER, we discussed microphones – argu-
ably the most important piece of podcasting gear you'll ever
own. It's the only way to get your voice into your listeners'
earbuds.

In this chapter, we're going to focus on the devices you'll need
in order to capture audio from your microphone. You won't
need both; just one or the other when you're starting out.

AUDIO INTERFACES

An audio interface is a device that turns the audio signals from
your microphone into data your computer can store and process digitally.

It takes what's called analog audio and converts it into digital
audio – long strings of ones and zeros that can be stored in
computer memory and saved to your hard drive.

And when you play your recording back from your hard drive, the interface works in the opposite direction and turns those ones and zeros back into analog audio you can hear through your headphones or speakers. Pretty cool, huh?

An audio interface almost always has a small desktop box that connects to your computer with some kind of cable but they come in a few different flavors.

There are more expensive interfaces that require you to install an expansion card inside your computer. These are usually fast and reliable but tend to have a lot more inputs – not to mention a higher cost – than you'll need as someone who's new to podcasting.

Next, there are interfaces that connect over either FireWire or Thunderbolt. FireWire is becoming more difficult to find since *Apple* is no longer including that type of connectivity in their computers. FireWire can also be tricky when it comes to driver software. It's probably not the best choice for a new podcaster.

Thunderbolt is the new kid on the block. Audio interfaces with Thunderbolt are still on the expensive side but that will change over time. And because the technology is still relatively new, driver software might be a little sketchy for some computer operating systems.

Last but not least, there's USB. USB technology has been around for well over a decade. It's stable, well-known and driver support is usually very good. There are plenty of options available from well-known manufacturers and you don't have to spend a ton of money to get a good one.

A USB audio interface is normally the best bet for a new podcaster.

Some of the models I recommend include:

- Focusrite Scarlett 2i2

- M-Audio M-Track

I've owned several M-Audio products over the years and they've been reliable and produced consistent, high-quality results. They're priced fairly and deliver great value.

Some things to consider when you're shopping for an audio interface include:

MICROPHONE PREAMPLIFIERS

The interfaces I've mentioned above all have built-in microphone preamplifiers. However, not all interfaces do. If a model you're considering doesn't make it clear, ask a salesperson or do some additional research.

NUMBER OF INPUTS

You can find interfaces with 8, 16 or 32 inputs. As you might expect, more inputs generally translate to a higher price tag.

As a general rule of thumb, your interface will need one input for every microphone you plan to record simultaneously. When you're starting out, it's unlikely you'll need more than two inputs for podcasting. So unless you plan to have multiple guests in the same room, all on separate microphones, you'll likely be fine with two inputs most of the time.

USB VERSION

Avoid USB 1.1. It's an old technology. Thankfully, there aren't many v1.1 devices left on the market. But if an interface is freakishly cheap (or there's a lot of dust on the box) ask about the USB version. Version 1.1 is not really fast enough to record and playback audio reliably. Look for a USB 2.0 device. The product description should tell you the version.

USB went to version 3.0 recently so we'll be seeing more and more USB 3.0 interfaces in the future. For the time being v2.0 will meet your needs 99% of the time.

> **Note***: With many of the better USB audio interfaces, you'll receive Digital Audio Workstation (DAW) software included in the box. It's usually a stripped-down or "lite" version of the manufacturer's flagship software. It's also common for the "lite" version to offer you a discount on the full-featured "pro" version when you're ready to upgrade. So, it's a good deal all around.*

REMINDER

An interface doesn't do much on its own. It has to be connected to either a Mac or Windows PC in order to record your podcast audio. This may sound like a down side but it really isn't. It's how most audio recording has been done in professional studios for the better part of two decades.

AUDIO RECORDERS

An audio recorder is a very different beast than an audio interface. Admittedly, there are similarities. They both turn analog audio into digital audio. They generally both have microphone preamplifiers, headphone outputs and some sort of recording meters.

But unlike an interface, an audio recorder is a completely stand-alone piece of gear. It doesn't need to be connected to a computer to record audio.

Other differences include: A recorder can run on batteries. It records audio to a memory card (rather than a hard drive). And many of the recorders on the market right now are small enough to fit in the palm of your hand.

Some of the models I recommend are:

- Tascam DR-100mkii

- Zoom H4n

Note: *I own the Tascam DR-100mkii and it's been great.*

I haven't used the Zoom myself but it's very popular among many podcasters and independent filmmakers and it's cheaper than the Tascam model.

With an audio recorder, you plug your microphone into the XLR connection, adjust the preamp level, hit record and you're off to the races.

And because it's battery-powered, you can record your podcast pretty much anywhere – in the back seat of a car, in a closet, on the street, in a forest. Anywhere.

Once you've recorded your podcast, you'll need to pop the memory card out of your recorder, load the audio files onto your computer, then edit and process them.

Note: Many recorders allow file transfer over USB so you may never actually have to remove the memory card from your device.

As you've guessed, the recorder offers a lot of flexibility.

INTERFACE OR RECORDER?

So which one to buy? I know you've heard this answer before but, *it depends*:

- It depends on your budget.

- It depends on the kind of podcast you want to produce.

- It depends on whether you need to be mobile.

- It depends on the type of computer you have.

IMPORTANT NOTE

If you're producing a podcast, you'll almost always need to edit your audio after you record it. And editing can only be done with software on a computer (either a Mac or Windows PC). So even if you use a recorder, I'm afraid there's no getting around it – you will still need access to a computer.

RECOMMENDATION

If you're an experienced podcaster and have a decent budget, consider buying both an interface and a recorder. You can use the interface at home and the recorder when you're on the road. It's good to have options. Also, if you own both devices, you can set them up to record at the same time. That way, if your computer happens to crash or otherwise fail in the middle of a session, the battery-powered recorder will have a back-up copy on memory card.

However, if you're starting out, have a limited budget or don't really know the type of podcast you're going to produce, I recommend purchasing one of the audio recorders listed in this section. A recorder will give you the most flexibility. You can carry it around, power it with batteries and not have to worry about computer crashes while you're recording.

WHAT ABOUT USB MICROPHONES?

You may be wondering, *"What about USB microphones? Do they need an interface?"*

Excellent question!

A USB microphone has an audio interface built into the microphone body. So, if you're using a USB mic (like the ATR2100 we covered in Chapter 2), you don't need a separate interface or recorder. You can simply plug it into your computer, load your recording software and start recording.

Not bad, huh?

ASSIGNMENT #3

BUY AN INTERFACE OR RECORDER

As a reminder, when you're starting out, you won't need both an interface and a recorder – just one or the other.

Based on my recommendations earlier in the chapter, decide how much you can afford to spend, where and how you intend to record your podcast, then make your purchase.

As always, do some research of your own to be sure you make an educated decision – but don't overdo it.

Nail down a single device. Buy it. And get ready to record!

[4]

Recording and Editing Software

RECORDING AND EDITING are two very distinct and different parts of the podcasting creation process.

Recording refers to the step in which you capture the audio from your microphone and store it either:

1. To your computer's hard-drive: if you record through an audio interface; or

2. To a memory card: if you record with an audio recorder.

On the other hand, *editing* refers to what you do with the audio data once it's been recorded. As you've probably guessed, you have to record audio before you can edit it.

The good news is that you generally won't need separate software packages to record and edit. Most modern audio software is capable of performing both functions. The software used for these purposes is called Digital Audio Workstation or DAW software.

DAWs take care of the hard work: talking to your audio interface (or USB microphone), storing audio and configuration files to disk, and performing editing and processing functions.

There are a number of DAW packages available with prices ranging from free to thousands of dollars. My advice for new podcasters remains the same:

Use hardware and software that is as close to free as possible without sacrificing quality or making your life too difficult. To satisfy both of these conditions, you'll generally find the sweet spot is somewhere between free and expensive. Let's look at the options.

FREE SOFTWARE

AUDACITY (WINDOWS, MAC & LINUX)

Audacity can perform most of the basic recording, editing and processing functions you need to produce a podcast. I've played with Audacity several times and have always found the interface less than intuitive. You can get things done but not always in the most efficient way. By all means, give Audacity a test drive. If it meets your needs, go with it. But in my opinion, there are better free or close-to-free options available.

GARAGE BAND (MAC-ONLY)

If you own an *Apple* computer, the next free option is Garage Band. Garage Band has the standard *Apple Computer* look-and-feel so it's easy to navigate and use. Definitely give Garage Band a shot if you're a Mac user. It may be all you need.

PRESONUS STUDIO ONE PRIME (MAC & WINDOWS)

The free version of PreSonus Studio One gives you the option to test drive the Pro version free for 30 days. As you'd expect, the free version has some limitations but it definitely has everything you'll need to produce your first podcast.

LOW-COST SOFTWARE

If you try out Audacity, Garage Band or Studio One and find they don't give you what you need, luckily there are some great low-cost options available. Here are a few:

CAKEWALK MUSIC CREATOR (WINDOWS-ONLY)

Music Creator is a full-fledged DAW so you can do a lot more than podcasting if you ever want to. It even has a touch-screen interface if you happen to own one of those fancy laptop/tablet hybrids. And it costs less than $50. It's definitely worth a look if you're a Windows user.

COCKOS REAPER (WINDOWS & MAC)

Reaper is powerful DAW software with a free 60-day evaluation period and a $60 price tag. It's a great value and will give you all the recording, editing and processing tools you'll need now and in the future.

SUMMARY

As with all software, I encourage you to try-before-you-buy. Most manufacturers offer a free trial period – usually 30-days. So definitely take advantage of that if it's available.

The choice between free, low-cost and high-cost is something you'll have to decide based on your budget. If you go the paid route, it's a good idea to buy into a family of products that offers you room to grow into a pro version if you ever need to.

It's also common for free or lite versions of DAW software to offer discounted upgrades to pro versions. So there's a real financial benefit to buying into a family of products you like.

In any event, don't stress too much over DAW software. The important things are:

1. you pick one; and

2. you start using it

If your budget is tight, start with free software today. You may need a package with greater functionality six months or a year from now and that's fine. But the sooner you start playing around with DAW software, the sooner you'll get your podcast out into the world. And that's exactly what you're aiming for, right?

Assignment #4

Choose a DAW Package

1. Pick out a DAW software package – free or low-cost depending on your budget.

2. Record something. Record anything. It can be yourself reading, your kids singing, your spouse snoring. Anything at all!

What you record at this point isn't important. What is important is that you become comfortable using the software.

Your first recording session will likely take far too long and produce a less than great result. It doesn't matter. What's important is that you do it. Your second session will be twice as good and take half the time. The third will be better yet. Get the bad ones out of the way so no one hears them but you. There's good stuff coming; just be patient.

[5]

Must-Have Accessories

THE TERMS *MUST-HAVE* and *accessories* seem to contradict one another. Let me explain.

If you have exactly zero dollars to spend and no way of borrowing, begging or stealing a few extra bucks to purchase the items we discuss in this chapter, the world won't end. You'll still be able to record and produce your podcast. And you should. Recording without accessories is a far better idea than not recording at all.

But the accessories we're going to discuss in this chapter are products that will take your podcast quality from *good* to *great*. And at the same time, they won't require a huge financial investment.

Here they are, in no particular order:

MICROPHONE STAND

Yes, it is possible to hold your microphone in your hand. And in a pinch, you can get away with that. But think about the following:

The average podcast is approximately 30 minutes long. Some shows – Dan Carlin's *Hardcore History* for example – can be over four hours per episode. Do you really want to hold a microphone to your face for four hours? Trust me, you don't.

Not only is your arm going to get painfully tired, but every time you shift your hand on the microphone body, the sound it produces (known as *handling noise*) is going to end up on your podcast. And those noises will make your podcast sound less professional.

Don't let that happen. Get yourself an inexpensive mic stand. For under $20, you'll solve two problems: 1) You'll prevent your arm from feeling like you've pitched nine innings; and 2) Your podcast won't contain distracting, unprofessional handling noise.

There are literally hundreds of different makes and models of microphone stands available. Don't stress the selection process too much.

If you have both floor space and storage space, a floor stand with a boom arm is a great choice. The boom will allow you to adjust the microphone position to almost any imaginable height and angle. You won't need to spend more than $25 to get a solid starter model.

If you have a small room and/or little storage space, consider a desk-top mic stand. This will sit on your desk or table and adjust to a comfortable height while you're seated. You can purchase a decent model for $20 or less.

SHOCK MOUNT

Remember those hand vibrations we talked about a moment ago? Well it's not just hand vibrations you need to worry about. It's also footsteps, computer key presses, air conditioning, and heavy vehicles passing by on the street outside your home.

Even if your mic is on a proper stand, it's still possible to pick up vibrations from both inside and outside your recording room. A shock mount uses elastic bands to physically isolate your microphone from the stand it's attached to. Any vibrations that reach the stand are absorbed by the elastic and never make it to the microphone.

Shock mounts can be expensive but you don't need an expensive one when you're starting out. Just be certain the one you buy fits the diameter of your microphone.

POP FILTER

Whenever your mouth makes a 'P' sound (and sometimes 'T' and 'B' sounds), it creates a small gust of air called a *plosive*. When humans speak to one another without a microphone, we hear only the 'P', not the gust.

Here's an experiment:

Hold your hand two inches from your mouth and say the following sentence:

"This is a short sentence."

Did you feel any air bursts against your hand? Maybe a little, but not much, right?

Now hold your hand in the same position and say this:

"Peter prefers peppers on pizza."

There's a big difference with this second sentence, right?

All of those tiny bursts of air you felt against your hand sound like huge explosions against a microphone's diaphragm. They're distracting, and when they're frequent, they can make your podcast sound amateur-ish. And because plosives can be completely banished cheaply and easily, there's no need to risk sounding like an amateur.

Attach a pop filter to your microphone stand and adjust it so it's approximately two inches away from the front of your microphone. And for about $10, you've gotten rid of the plosive problem – pretty much once and for all. That's money well-spent.

There are more expensive pop filters available but there's really no need to spend any more than $10 or $12.

XLR CABLES

If you buy a non-USB microphone, it will require a preamp. And if your microphone requires a preamp, you'll need a cable to connect it to your audio interface or recorder. XLR refers to the three-pin, locking connectors on either end of the cable. These connectors and cables are important because the devices you connect on either end use the signals on each of the three pins to keep noise levels to a minimum.

> **Note:** *If the microphone you're considering doesn't have an XLR connector, it may not be the best microphone for podcasting. I encourage you to consider other XLR mic options.*

If you spend any time around audio people, they can be very particular about their cables. Some only use a specific brand. Others are willing to spend $10 per foot for custom, handmade cables. My advice: don't listen to these people.

Cables are important but don't let a salesperson, audiophile friend or anyone else convince you a microphone cable has to be any particular brand or contain any minimum percentage of gold.

Buy a decent cable. Don't over spend. Don't under spend. Look for cables with *Neutrik* brand XLR connectors as they have a reputation for quality, durability and performance.

One thing to remember is that audio signals lose strength over longer cable runs. So if you only need a 10-foot cable, don't buy a 50-foot cable. A 15-footer will do just fine and give you a little slack in case you need to move around.

HEADPHONES

This is one piece of gear that's easy to forget. But it's super important.

Have you ever wondered why people in broadcasting studios and radio stations wear headphones?

They're all sitting in the same room, right? They should be able to hear one another the same way they would at a dinner table. They probably can, but that's not the point. The point is that unless you're hearing your voice through headphones as you speak, there's a good chance your microphone technique is going to suffer.

Microphone technique is a topic we'll cover in greater detail in the next chapter. For the moment, the point to remember is that whenever you speak into a microphone, you should be monitoring (that is, *listening to*) yourself through headphones.

This accomplishes three things:

1. Hearing your voice as you speak ensures your mouth doesn't wander too far from the microphone while recording.

2. If your interface or recorder fails during a recording, you'll most likely stop hearing your voice through your headphones and you will be able to address the situation immediately.

3. With headphones covering your ears, the only way you can hear the other people in the room is – you guessed it – through headphones.

In case you're wondering, earbud-style headphones really won't cut it for recording. To monitor properly, you'll need over-the-ear, closed-back headphones. This style has large speaker drivers so you can hear things clearly and the closed-back feature ensures very little of what you're hearing bleeds out into your microphone.

You can find a decent set of headphones meeting all these requirements for as little as $20 and – while more expensive headphones do exist – you don't need to spend more than $80 (or so) for the industry-standard Sony MDR-7506.

> **Note**: *My advice is to stay away from wireless headphones for podcast monitoring. Nothing beats a hardwired cable for quality, reliability and simplicity.*

ASSIGNMENT #5

BUY MUST-HAVE ACCESSORIES

I have a strong suspicion you're committed to creating a great podcast. Otherwise, it's doubtful you would have purchased this book and still be reading after five chapters. And because you've stuck with me, I also suspect you care about quality.

So today's assignment is to go shopping and get yourself the accessories I've discussed in this chapter. If you own one or more of these items already, excellent. If you can beg, borrow or steal one or more items from a friend or family member, do it. If you can find previously-enjoyed gear on eBay at a huge discount off its retail price, grab it.

How you build your kit isn't all that important. What's important is that you build it. See the note below for details on a tremendous offer I believe will help you get started with the least amount of time, energy and money.

Note: *To help you build your podcasting kit with a minimum of effort, I'm offering owners of this book a steep discount on my **Master Podcasters' Gear Guide**. It's is a no-brainer purchase at this price. Here's the link to the discount offer:*

http://masterpodcaster.com/gearguide-discount

[6]

Microphone Technique

A T THIS POINT, we're almost half-way through the book, so it's time for a quick summary.

Back in Chapter 2, we learned about the different types of microphones and which ones are best-suited to podcast recording in rooms that don't sound so great. That lead to an understanding of why I recommend dynamic microphones over condenser microphones for podcasting.

As a refresher, here are the four microphones I recommend from most expensive to least:

1. Shure SM7B

2. Heil Sound PR 40

3.   Shure SM58

4.   Audio-Technica ATR2100

All four of these microphones are *dynamic* types.

The first three require a preamp which means you'll need to plug them into an audio interface, recorder or mixer. The fourth microphone (the ATR2100) is a USB dynamic that can plug directly into a USB port on your computer. However, the ATR2100 can also connect to an interface or recorder if you choose to use it that way. That's an important point to remember.

Ready for a quiz? It's multiple choice, and there's only one correct answer. Here's the question:

> **To create a pro-quality podcast recording, your microphone should be:**
>
> *a) in a proper shock mount*
>
> *b) on a mic stand*
>
> *c) mounted behind a pop filter*
>
> *d) connected to your interface or recorder using a good (but not-too-expensive) XLR cable*
>
> *e) all of the above*

Think about it for a minute. Got your answer?

Alright!

If you chose *e) all of the above*, you're a winner. See how much you've learned in only five short chapters?

Now that you're approaching expert status at setting up podcasting gear, let's make sure you're using it properly.

This is where the rubber meets the road. It's where you finally step up to the microphone (literally). Take a deep breath. And speak loud and clear into the ears of the nation. No, make that "the ears of the world!" It's really not that hard. There are just a few techniques you need to be aware of and practice until you've mastered them.

Don't expect your first try at this to sound amazing. It won't. Not unless you're very lucky or have very low standards. And since you're reading this book by choice, I'm assuming your standards are high.

Here are some of the most important microphone techniques:

MICROPHONE PLACEMENT

Dynamic microphones aren't incredibly sensitive. It's the main reason I recommend them for podcasting. They don't pick up sounds that are more than a few inches away from their diaphragms (i.e. the part of the microphone that moves when you speak.) To capture a good, quiet recording, your mouth has to be close to the microphone.

How close? Good question.

If you recall our *Accessories* discussion in the last chapter, you know your pop filter will be about two inches from the front of your microphone. And your mouth should be two to four inches in front of the pop filter. So in total, your mouth will be between four to six inches away from the microphone.

> **Note:** *As a general rule, closer is almost always better when it comes to dynamic microphone placement. But try to avoid being so close that your lips are touching the pop filter.*

You'll need to experiment to find the perfect distance for your voice. The perfect distance will depend on a couple of factors:

PROXIMITY EFFECT

The closer you are to the microphone, the deeper your voice will sound. This is called *proximity effect.* Here's a link to a Wikipedia article on this topic.

> **Proximity Effect:**
>
> *http://masterpodcaster.com/wiki-proximity*

The short explanation is that the closer a sound source is to a microphone, the more pronounced the low frequencies are. And low frequencies are what make your voice sound deep.

Experiment with this: Find a distance that makes your voice sound most flattering and natural and make a mental note of that placement so you can repeat it in future recording sessions.

YOUR PREAMP GAIN SETTING

When you record, you'll need to adjust your preamp gain setting so the blinking lights average around the two-thirds level. This is usually -12 decibels (dB) on what's known as the *VU meter.*

If you record much below this level, you may have to add volume in your DAW software later. This typically adds noise. And noise should be avoided whenever possible. If you record much above the -12dB level, you run the risk of clipping. You'll know clipping when you hear it. It sounds terrible and is almost impossible to fix after the fact.

Your VU meter will bounce around a lot as you record. But, always try to keep your average level close to -12dB. That's the *Goldilocks* level. It's just right.

> *Note: In a quiet environment, your VU meter should be completely dark (i.e. no lights blinking) when you're not speaking. The recommended average level of -12dB applies only while you're speaking – not the average between speaking and non-speaking levels.*

As you experiment, you'll notice that the average VU meter reading changes with your distance from the microphone. When you're speaking at the same volume, your VU meter will register higher as you move closer to the microphone and lower as you move further away.

You can always increase the gain of your preamp but when you do that, you also increase the level of any noises you don't want to hear. If you recall, these include sounds such as:

- Your computer fan

- Your keyboard key presses

- The television in the next room

- Traffic noise, etc.

My advice here is to take the Carnegie Hall approach: Practice. Practice. Practice.

Record yourself reading from a book or talking to your spouse or kids. In fact, record your spouse and kids. You'll learn a lot just by setting up a microphone and having someone else speak into it. Different people speak at different volumes so you'll get to see what kind of preamp and microphone placement changes are necessary when you record people other than yourself.

But definitely record your own voice too. After all, your voice is always available where and when you are.

Mouth Noises

It's important to pay attention to the sounds your mouth makes when you speak into a microphone. Because you're only a few inches away, the microphone will hear a lot more of the quiet noises your mouth makes than will a conversation partner who's several feet away.

Some noises you may notice the first few times you record your own voice include:

Plosives ('P' sounds)

At this point, I hope I've convinced you to use a pop filter every time you record. But even if you always work with a pop filter, there's only so much wind a microphone can handle.

If you're a loud talker whose Ps, Bs or Ts are very aggressive, you may find you need more protection than a pop filter offers. This is where good technique comes in. Here's what you need to do: Instead of pointing the microphone directly at your mouth, turn it approximately 30 degrees off-axis. The microphone should still be pointed toward your mouth but just slightly off center. By doing this, bursts of wind that leave your lips slide along the microphone diaphragm rather than bouncing directly off of it. This helps reduce plosive volumes to acceptable levels.

Try several different angles to find which works best for you. At the same time, always keep the microphone within four to six inches of your mouth. As you change the microphone angle, you may need to increase the gain of your preamp to keep your VU meter averaging -12dB. Increasing the gain slightly is okay, just don't overdo it.

SMACKS, CRACKLES AND POPS

No, this section isn't about breakfast cereal.

You may notice your mouth makes crackling or smacking noises when you speak. This is something almost no one notices about themselves until they record and listen to their own voice. These sounds can be caused by your tongue against the roof of your mouth, your lips breaking suction as you open them or the interior of your mouth sticking together because it's dry. Whatever the cause, here's my advice:

1. If you hear smacks, crackles or clicks very infrequently – a few per minute or so – don't worry about it. Most human beings make sounds like this and if yours aren't too loud or too frequent, it's likely your audience will never notice them.

2. If, however, you hear them every time you open your mouth, it's probably going to be distracting to a podcast listener.

If dry mouth is the culprit, keep a bottle or glass of water at your side at all times. Sip it frequently and stay hydrated. This will help a lot.

If your mouth sounds aren't the result of dry mouth, you're going to need to learn some new skills. Start by paying close attention to the sounds you make when you speak – how your tongue touches different parts of your mouth, how your lips smack or pop when you start a sentence and anything else that produces a distracting noise.

Once you're aware of what's causing the noises, you'll be in a much better position to adjust the way you speak so these *bad* sounds are less loud and less frequent.

HEAVY BREATHING

No... not *that* type of heavy breathing.

Frequent and loud breath sounds can be very distracting to a podcast listener. Like other sounds discussed in this chapter, one or two breaths here or there isn't something you should be concerned about. But if you can hear every breath you take (No *Police* jokes, please!) through your microphone, you may need to change things up.

Since not breathing at all is an all-around bad idea, you'll need to learn to breathe more quietly. Sometimes a change as simple as inhaling through your nose rather than through your mouth is all you need. If that doesn't work, try taking less intense but more frequent breaths and see if that helps.

As with other mouth noise issues, becoming conscious of your breath and experimenting with different solutions is the best advice.

While it's always preferable to avoid recording breath sounds in the first place, once they're on your hard drive or memory card, changing your breathing technique won't help. In these situations, there are DAW software plugins available that will help. A processing plugin known as an **expander** can be used to reduce the volume of breath sounds (and any other low volume sounds) that happen between words. As with most plugins, an expander requires careful configuration for each situation. I generally recommend solving recording problems at the source rather than relying on software to fix them after the fact. But it's good to know an expander is an option if you ever get stuck.

FILLERS

The next time you're engaged in a conversation, pay close attention. Chances are good you'll hear your partner (and maybe even yourself) say at least a single *uhm*, *ah*, *like* or *ya-know* in almost every sentence. These are known as fillers. Again, they're commonplace in conversation but can become distracting and unprofessional if overused.

Professional podcasters, broadcasters, voice over artists and public speakers train themselves to avoid using fillers. If they can do it, so can you. Practice. Practice. Practice.

ASSIGNMENT #6

ANALYZE YOUR MICROPHONE TECHNIQUE

Pick a phrase you can memorize without too much effort: a song lyric, a poem, a nursery rhyme – anything will do.

Set up your microphone and start recording.

Repeat the phrase a dozen or more times.

Each time you repeat it, make a slight change to one of the following variables:

1. Your distance from the microphone

2. The angle of the microphone

3. The gain on your interface, recorder or microphone preamp

4. Your plosives – Try making your Ps less forceful (and more forceful so you'll have a basis for comparison)

5. Mouth sounds – Smacks, crackles, pops and breathing noises

When you're done, play them back and listen closely for the differences. These experiments will make you more familiar with how your voice sounds when recorded. It will also help you control key aspects of your performance so you'll be able to consistently produce high-quality recordings when it counts.

[7]

Audio Editing

I N THIS CHAPTER, we're going to discuss two specific audio editing techniques. They're not super-advanced techniques. In fact, they're quite basic. But I'm being very fair in referring to them as *the most important* editing techniques.

Before we dive into the meat of the chapter, I want to take a quick moment and discuss why podcast editing is necessary.

This may be a bold statement but I'm going to say that never in the history of humankind has a podcast been recorded that could not be improved with editing. You've likely heard podcasts that contained weird sounds or mispronounced words or Skype data delays or long pauses or something else distracting. Here's an example I encountered not too long ago.

UNNECESSARY (PODCAST) ROUGHNESS

Several months back, I was listening to a podcast interview by a lovely lady who specializes in Facebook advertising.

She was interviewing a very popular Internet Marketer who shared his background and the story of how he'd reached his current level of success. It was an interesting interview. I chuckled a few times. And I learned some things I was happy to learn. On top of that, the audio quality was fantastic. This lady really knows what she's doing with a microphone.

The interview was great until this happened:

> *Guest: "... his business is six-figures and..."*
>
> *Host: "Oh. We lost you again. Hold on. Let me see if you come back. Can you hear me?"*
>
> *Guest: "Amy? Ya got me?"*
>
> *Host: "Okay. Now. So, this is where I lost you. You said he went on to build..."*

That exchange was likely the result of a Skype drop-out. That's not uncommon. Skype drop-outs happen all the time, and more often than not, they're completely beyond your control.

But there's absolutely no reason on earth for the final version of that podcast – the one the interviewer released to *iTunes* – to contain any of that, *"Can you hear me?"* banter. None of it. Removing that section from the episode would have required five or six keystrokes and taken 60 seconds to accomplish – two minutes at most.

Editing is a skill. And just like everything else worth doing, it takes time and effort to master. But editing is not difficult. And it's very much worth the time and effort.

So as you learn this craft of podcasting, I encourage you to think of editing as one additional tool you can use to make your show stand out from the others whose hosts aren't willing to spend the time and effort.

The golden rule of editing is this:

If you can improve your podcast by removing something, DO IT. That *something* in your audio might be:

- Long pauses

- Excessive fillers (i.e. *uhms* and *ahhs*)

- Curse words (if your podcast is G-rated)

- Inaccurate information

- Inappropriate comments

These are examples. I'm certain you can think of others. The point is, the editing process gives you an opportunity to make the world right.

As soon as you load your audio tracks in your Digital Audio Workstation, you become the master of that universe. Each DAW will require a slightly different combination of key presses and mouse clicks but the process will be more or less the same in each.

In the walk-through that follows, I'm going to use the keyboard shortcuts from the Cakewalk family of DAW products because that's what I'm most familiar with. And... because it's my book.

TECHNIQUE #1: REMOVING AUDIO

Use this technique any time you want to completely remove a section of audio.

For example, you might want to remove a long pause. Perhaps you stopped speaking to take a few sips of water. Don't subject your audience to those ten seconds of *dead air*. Just cut it out.

Or perhaps an interview went off on a tangent and into an area that was boring, off-topic, or inappropriate for the audience. Lose it.

The bottom line is this: If there's any part of a recording you don't want to end up in your listeners' earbuds, you have the authority and control to remove it.

Once you've loaded the audio file into your DAW, here's how you do it:

1. Find the start of the section you want to remove.

2. Place your cursor on the audio clip at that point.

3. Press the 'S' key (i.e. 'S' for Split).

You'll now see the audio clip has been split into two sections.

Next:

4. Find the end of the section you want to remove.

5. Place your cursor there.

6. Press the 'S' key again.

The track is now in three sections. Let's keep going.

7. Click on the middle of the three clips. This should highlight the section you want to remove.

8. Click the *Delete* key.

At this point, the *bad* section (i.e. the one with the silence or the curse word or the racial slur) disappears.

Where'd it go? No one really knows. It's just gone. And it's not your problem anymore.

On your DAW screen, you should now have two audio clips separated by a blank region. Next comes the magical part.

9. Click and hold on the rightmost clip and use your mouse to drag it to the left until it butts up against the first clip.

Congratulations! You've just completed your first edit.

TECHNIQUE #2: ADDING SILENCE

You: *"Uhhhm... Adding wut now???"*

That's right. *Adding silence.* Sometimes it's necessary to add silence to your podcast. Let me explain. Here's a scenario:

You and your podcast guest are talking during a recorded interview when suddenly someone slams a door in the next room: just one, sudden bang. And then it's over.

You were focusing on the interview and didn't notice the door slam until you played the recording back later that day after the guest had left. The door slam happens between words so it doesn't interrupt the conversation. You're just stuck with a door slam right in the middle of an otherwise perfect interview.

What do you do?

Well, if you've been following this chapter closely up to this point, you're going to say, *"S key, S key, Delete key, Click, Drag, Done."*

If that was your answer, nice work – that's almost perfect. But then you'd play that section of audio back and discover the words on either side of the section you removed now sound too close together.

Remember, you just removed audio that would have otherwise been silence between words. And now those words are so close together, they seem rushed, awkward and unnatural.

What do you do now?

This is an advanced technique. But I'm certain you can handle it. The solution starts with finding a silent section of audio in your recording, copying it and pasting it *IN PLACE OF* the door slam you removed. If the silence you paste is the exact length of the section you removed, words on either side of it will sound natural – just the way they were originally recorded.

Pretty cool, huh?

In a Cakewalk DAW, you copy an audio section by splitting it at two points, clicking on it and pressing *Ctrl+C* (i.e. Copy). You can then paste it by putting your cursor at the destination position and clicking *Ctrl+V* (i.e. Paste).

If you need to, you can adjust the length of the silent clip by click-dragging the left and/or right edges of the clip until it fits nicely in the gap left by the door slam you removed.

PRO TIP

Any time you record – more importantly *anywhere* you record – always, always, always do this:

Set your microphone up in a comfortable recording position. Set your preamp gain level so your signal averages around -12dB when you're talking. Start to record. And...

Don't speak.

That's right.

Record silence.

For 30 seconds. 60 seconds if you can stand it. 10 seconds if that's all the time you have.

The pros call this silent recording *Room Tone*. You see, every room sounds different. Even the same room on different days – or at different times on the same day – can sound very different.

To ensure you have plenty of silence to work with during the editing process, always record room tone before or after every session. Trust me. You'll be glad you did.

ASSIGNMENT #7

PRACTICE ADDING AND REMOVING SILENCE

Open an audio file in your DAW software. Now, go back to the techniques outlined above and walk through each step by step.

1. Remove some audio from a recording.

2. Add silence to a recording using room tone you've recorded.

3. For extra credit, cut up a couple of recorded sentences and reorder the words. Create a sentence you didn't actually speak. Notice how the spacing of words and their intonation are crucial to making a sentence sound natural and believable.

4. Keep practicing.

[8]

Equalization

A COUPLE OF FUN FACTS before we get into the meat of the chapter.

> *Fact #1*: *Equalization is often referred to by its short name, EQ.*

> *Fact #2*: *Human beings can hear frequencies between 20Hz (i.e. the "low end") and 20,000Hz (i.e. the "high end"). As we age, we lose the ability to hear the higher frequencies – they're the first to go.*

I listen to a lot of podcasts. And because I have several decades' worth of recording experience, my ears can estimate fairly accurately how much time and effort the creator put into producing their podcast.

I sometimes hear shows that sound like they were recorded frantically, immediately converted to MP3 and released to *iTunes* – all within an hour.

But let me tell you something – no one is that good. No one in the history of humankind has recorded anything that wouldn't benefit HUGELY from the smallest amount of thoughtful production.

And podcast production doesn't need to take days. Depending on the recording, it may not even take hours. But it takes *some* time, and it's not that difficult.

The topics we're going to cover in this chapter and the next don't require super powers, thousands of dollars' worth of gear, or several days' worth of effort. You just need to understand why they're necessary, how and when to apply them and – like any other skill – practice them until they become second nature.

WHAT IS EQUALIZATION?

Have you ever owned or used a radio, stereo or music player that had knobs or sliders to adjust the Bass, Treble or Midrange? Those knobs are equalization controls.

The phones, tablets and media players we own today don't have knobs or sliders. But they almost always have EQ controls of some sort embedded several menu layers deep.

Bass, midrange and treble refer to different parts of the audio frequency spectrum.

Bass is on the low end. It has a name you're already familiar with. The bass range contains those sounds made by baritone voices, bass drums and bass guitars. You can sometimes *feel* these sounds in your chest when they play through big, amplified speakers.

Treble refers to the higher end of the frequency range. It's where things like lead guitar solos, cymbals and vocal sibilance (the sounds your mouth makes when you pronounce the letter 'S') exist.

Midrange is what's left over. It's everything in between the bass range and the treble range. This is where you find most of the information in an audio recording and virtually all the content of a spoken-word podcast. The human voice consists of frequencies mostly in the midrange.

Equalization is just a fancy, five-syllable word that refers to the process of adjusting the frequency content of your audio. Why would you do such a thing? The word *equalization* itself is a major clue to the answer.

At the risk of stating the obvious, equalization is used to *equalize* your audio recording – to ensure the bass, midrange and treble are properly-balanced against one another and that none of the ranges stick out in a distracting or unappealing way.

When it comes to equalization, there are very few hard and fast rules. This is because each podcast recording will sound different depending on factors that include:

- The character of your voice

- The room you record in

- The microphone you use

- Your microphone technique

- The preamps on your audio interface or recorder

- The speakers or headphones you monitor through

Even if you could control every one of these recording factors perfectly, you'd still have no control over how or where your audience is listening to your show. They may be listening:

- Through earbuds

- Through Dr. Dre Beats headphones

- On a home stereo

- In a perfectly quiet room

- On a noisy Manhattan sidewalk during rush hour

So what chance do you have of equalizing *the right way*? As I mentioned earlier, there are *few* hard and fast rules. Let's talk about those few.

Equalization "Rules"

Low End

Unless you're a baritone opera singer, your voice has very little content below 80Hz. In fact, very few adult men or women have any vocal frequencies below 100Hz.

On a vocal recording, the sounds that typically exist in this range are ones you don't want or need. They include things like:

- Air conditioning hum

- Traffic rumble

- Accidental thumps and bumps against your microphone cable or stand

So the obvious question is, *"If there's nothing useful in this range, why keep it?"* The answer is, *"Don't!"*

> **Note:** *Pretty much every DAW software package in existence has an equalizer either built-in or available as a VST plugin. There should be no need to buy any additional tools to follow the instructions in this chapter.*

The first thing I recommend for every vocal recording is to add a high-pass filter (sometimes known as a *low-cut* filter) on the track.

Next, set the frequency of the filter to 100Hz. This is known as the cutoff frequency. Now play back the audio and listen.

As it plays back, gradually change the cutoff frequency, moving it slightly above and below 100Hz to see where it sounds best.

If you can nudge the filter higher than 100Hz, do so. But stop the instant your voice starts to sound unnatural and back it off slightly.

HIGH END

Just as the human voice contains very little low end, it also contains very little audio information in the extreme high frequencies.

For most vocal recordings, what exists in the high end of the audible range are sounds you generally don't want to hear, including:

- Hiss from low-quality preamps

- Distorted sibilance (i.e. 'S' sounds) produced by low-quality condenser microphones

- Some computer fan noises

Combine these undesirable sounds with the fact that most adults can't hear much beyond 15kHz by the time they're in their 30s and you have a strong case for removing as much of the high end as you reasonably can.

So, in your DAW, add a low-pass (or *high-cut*) filter and start with a cutoff frequency of 16,000Hz. Next, play the audio track and gradually adjust the cutoff frequency up and down. Your goal is to set the cutoff as low as possible while keeping your voice sounding natural.

This High-Pass plus Low-Pass filter combo technique is something I advise performing on every podcast track you record. It amounts to getting rid of information you don't need while maintaining unharmed all the information you do.

In terms of EQ, there may be other frequencies you'll need to boost or cut to improve the quality of your recording. But those types of tweaks depend highly on your room, voice, microphone, etc. My advice is, if something in your recording sounds odd, play around with your EQ.

Boost a little here. Cut a little there. Experiment until you're comfortable identifying problems with your ears and knowing how to fix them with EQ.

If your DAW software accepts VST plugins (some free software doesn't) and you'd like to play around with a really great EQ, download this free bundle and install it on your computer.

Melda Productions Bundle:

http://masterpodcaster.com/meldafreebundle

This bundle contains a dozen or more plugins so you'll get a lot more than just an EQ. It's definitely worth the download.

ASSIGNMENT #8

ADD HIGH-PASS AND LOW-PASS FILTERS TO A RECORDING

1. Open up your DAW software and record a short clip of your voice.

2. Insert an EQ plugin on the track.

3. Add a high-pass filter at 100Hz.

4. Add a low-pass filter at 16kHz.

5. Gradually adjust the cutoff frequency of each filter.

6. Move the high-pass frequency as *high* as you can without making your voice sound thin.

7. Move the low-pass frequency as *low* as you can without making your voice sound muddy.

If the terms *thin* and *muddy* in this context don't make sense to you right now, they will once you hear them.

FOR EXTRA CREDIT...

Research how to create a template in your DAW package so that every audio track you add to a project has both a high-pass and a low-pass filter enabled at your desired cutoff frequencies. Save this configuration as a template and you've immediately improved your podcasting workflow – saving yourself a minute or more each time you record a vocal track.

You're welcome.

[9]

Compression

I DON'T THINK I'M EXAGGERATING at all when I say compression is the one technique that separates the pros from the amateurs in the podcasting world.

It's not that podcasters don't know compression exists. It has more to do with the fact they don't know how to use it properly. They either under use it, so it's not really doing anything, or they overdo it and their podcast ends up sounding awful.

After this chapter, you'll be in the *Goldilocks Zone*. Not too much compression. Not too little. Just right.

The human voice is a dynamic instrument: *we can whisper;* **WE CAN SHOUT!**

But we spend most of our time somewhere in between – speaking at an average level.

But even within that *average* range, we vary our volume all the time. When we're making an important point, we speak a little louder. We sometimes tail off close to the end of a long sentence as we run out of breath. If we're emphasizing a word, that word ends up being louder. If we're embarrassed or sad or tired, we talk more quietly. You get the picture.

In the world of audio production, the difference between the quietest sound and the loudest sound on a given audio track is called the *Dynamic Range* or DR. The human voice has a fairly wide DR.

When someone downloads your podcast, queues it up on their player and plugs in their earbuds, you want them to hear every word you say. That should be easy to achieve but it's often not. The problem is that people rarely listen to podcasts under ideal conditions.

For instance, on my commute to work, I hear:

- Trucks passing by

- Subway trains entering the station

- Announcements on PA systems

- Loud (and sometimes *crazy*) people talking

The point is, if the podcast I'm listening to isn't compressed at all, I hear the loud words just fine. But I completely miss the softer ones. And this often has me hitting the rewind button to go back and hear what I've missed. And sometimes I don't hear the soft words the second time through. So I get frustrated, and feeling frustrated first thing in the morning is no fun.

All this is to say, with a little know-how, you can avoid making me frustrated. But (much) more importantly, by using compression effectively, you can avoid frustrating thousands of your podcast's dedicated listeners.

How do you do that? I'm glad you asked. You start by opening up your DAW, loading your podcast project and adding a compressor plugin to your vocal track. Pretty much every DAW has a built-in compressor plugin, so there's no need to spend extra bucks on one just yet.

If your DAW or recording package doesn't have a built-in compressor, here (again) is the link to a seriously great set of plugins you can download and use for the low, low price of zero dollars:

Melda Productions Bundle:

http://masterpodcaster.com/meldafreebundle

The Melda Productions bundle is one hundred percent free with no expiry and no nag screens. And if you care to, for a small upgrade fee you'll receive access to a bunch of additional features. I've used the plugins in this bundle dozens of times and I highly recommend them.

COMPRESSOR CONTROLS

Depending on the make and model of the compressor you use, it may have different controls and/or different control names than the ones I discuss in this section. Even if this is the case, you should be able to follow the steps I outline without much trouble.

The parameters you need to be concerned with right now are:

THRESHOLD

This is the level at which the compressor starts to compress. If your vocal signal never rises above the threshold level, the compressor has no effect at all on your audio. But if you set your threshold too low, the compressor will always be engaged and your vocal track will likely sound distorted or unnatural. Therefore, when you set the threshold level, you want to avoid both the *too high* and the *too low* scenarios.

RATIO

This is the amount the vocal signal is reduced in volume once it exceeds the threshold you've set. A ratio of 1:1 means the output signal is identical to the input signal. It means no compression is happening – even if the input signal is above the threshold. A high ratio (10:1 for example) is generally too much for a podcast vocal unless your intention is to use the compressor as a *limiter*.

> **Note**: *We'll discuss limiters in the next chapter. For right now, all you need to know is a limiter prevents a signal from exceeding a maximum level.*

For podcasting, you'll want to set a ratio of no more than 2:1. If you go much higher, your voice can start to sound unnatural. And unnatural is not what you want. A ratio of 2:1 means any time the input signal crosses the compressor's Threshold, its volume is cut in half. A signal that's six decibels above the threshold is reduced by three decibels. A signal that's two decibels above is reduced by one decibel.

OTHER PARAMETERS

Depending on how sophisticated your compressor plugin is, it may have some or all of the following additional parameters:

- *Attack Time* – The amount of time the compressor takes to *start* compressing after the signal *exceeds* the threshold level.

- *Release Time* – The amount of time the compressor takes to *stop* compressing after the signal drops *below* the threshold level.

- *Knee Shape* – Impacts whether compression begins abruptly at the threshold level or eases in gently before the threshold is crossed.

- *Peak / RMS Detection* – Determines whether the compressor reacts only to signal peaks or to an average of the signal energy over a longer period of time.

Each of these parameters changes how the compressor works in slightly different ways. But at this point in your compression education, don't be overly concerned. By all means, experiment with them at your leisure but leave them at default values for the purposes of this chapter.

HOW IT'S DONE

Let's compress. Set up your plugin according to these steps:

1. Threshold: Set this to -6dB as a starting point. We'll come back and adjust it in a minute.

2. Set your Ratio to 2:1.

3. Turn Auto-Gain off: This is important. You definitely want this OFF! If your compressor has no auto gain switch or checkbox, you can ignore this step.

> *Note: Auto-Gain attempts to help you by guessing how much louder the signal should be after compression takes place. The problem is, most auto-gain settings don't guess all that well. It's better to turn auto-gain off and adjust the gain level manually.*

4. Play your audio.

5. As audio plays back, begin slowly lowering the *Threshold* setting. As you move it lower, watch the *Gain Reduction* meter. This will usually be in the form of a glowing light, a bar or sometimes just an on-screen number – usually red in color. If available, it's the number you want to focus on.

6. As you lower the *Threshold*, you'll notice the higher volume sections of audio make the gain reduction meter light up (or change color). Continue lowering the *Threshold* until the loudest sections of your audio make the gain reduction meter read somewhere close to -3dB. It can be a little more or a little less; -3dB is just a target.

7. Next, increase the compressor's *Makeup Gain* by 3dB.

> **Note:** *Sometimes Makeup Gain is labeled Output Level or something similar. This is the control you want to increase.*

8. Stop audio playback. Rewind and play the track again from the beginning.

9. Take close notice of how the audio sounds. Are all the words clearly audible? Are there distorted sections?

Let's recap what we've done here:

1. Set the compressor up to reduce the volume of the loudest sections by three decibels.

2. Increased the overall volume level of the track by three decibels.

It almost seems as if *step 2* reverses *step 1* which wouldn't make sense. Think about it this way:

The compressor doesn't affect audio signals below the threshold. Those are left unchanged. So when we reduce the volume of only the loud parts by three decibels and then raise the overall volume of the entire track by three decibels, we're returning the loud parts of the recording to their original levels.

But – and this is the important part – the quieter parts of the track are now three decibels higher in volume. So, we've made the quiet parts louder while keeping the louder parts at the same volume. We've reduced the dynamic range of the track by three decibels. That's the magic a compressor performs.

Now, with this compression technique in your arsenal, when I listen to your podcast while riding the New York City subway and a voice on the PA system tells me, *"The next stop is Fulton Street. Transfer is available to the A, C, 4, 5, blah, blah"*, I'll still be able to hear the quieter parts of the jokes or instructions or opinions you're piping into my ears. And I won't be frustrated. Nor will your other listeners. Nice work.

ASSIGNMENT #9

SET UP A COMPRESSOR

Today's assignment is another practice exercise.

1. Set up your recording software, insert a compressor plugin and record yourself saying something. Saying anything.

2. Put your playback on infinite loop and start adjusting the compressor controls.

3. Focus mainly on the ratio and threshold – these are the two most critical parameters.

4. Notice how changes to each parameter affect how your recorded voice sounds.

5. Find a nice, natural balance and take note of the settings. Use them as a starting point for your next recording.

6. Add this compressor configuration to your template along with your low-pass and high-pass EQ filters.

[10]

Mastering

IF YOU'RE NOT FAMILIAR with the term, *mastering* refers to taking the final, edited, EQ-ed and compressed version of your podcast and putting one final polish on it before you send it out the door and into your listeners' earbuds.

WHY MASTERING IS NECESSARY

When you create a podcast episode, it will typically contain some or all of the following sections:

1. An intro with music and voice over (sometimes called a *bumper*)

2. An episode or show overview in which the host introduces the topic or the guest before the show begins

3. The show content itself

4. A recap in which the host points out important or noteworthy parts of the show or maybe discusses the topic or guest of the next episode

5. An outro bumper with music and voice over

Depending on your budget, your audience and your experience level, you may have fewer sections than this in your episodes. In fact, the only mandatory section is number 3 – the show itself. This is the only real part listeners are tuning in to hear. Everything else is optional.

But let's say you're an experienced professional with a decent budget and your show has all five sections. It's not uncommon for each section to be recorded:

- On different days

- Or with different gear

- Or by different people

- And at different volume levels

You've likely dealt with the volume levels of each section during the editing stage (sometimes referred to as *mixing*). During mixing, you place each audio section on its own DAW track and adjust the levels so each track's VU meter averages roughly the same level throughout the show.

In the mastering phase, you take the mixed project; add some additional compression, some gentle limiting and then render the final project out to a WAV format master file.

> **Note**: *It's important your master is in WAV format. WAV files are uncompressed. They're typically large but they're the highest quality audio you can produce. You want to keep all of your podcast audio in WAV format throughout all stages of production.*

So, how exactly do you get from *mix* to *master*? Let's discuss.

BUSS COMPRESSION

If you've set up your DAW properly, it will have a Master Buss. This is a final fader through which all the audio in your podcast episode is mixed before reaching your speakers or headphones. The master buss gives you one last opportunity to process the audio before it's sent out of your DAW. It may be labeled *Main* or *2-Buss* or something similar. Whatever it's called, locate it and add a compressor plugin.

> **Note**: *There are thousands of buss compressor plugins available on the market. Some can cost thousands of dollars. At this point in your podcasting career, pretty much any compressor will do. Even the same make and model you used on your recorded vocal during the Mix stage.*

So load that freebie compressor up and insert it on your master buss. You do have a freebie compressor, don't you? Just in case you missed it the first two times, here's the link to the Melda Productions bundle. One. More. Time.

Melda Production Free Effects Bundle:

http://masterpodcaster.com/meldafreebundle

The process we're going to follow here is almost identical to the process we covered in the last chapter. I'll recap it here:

Note: Before we begin, if your compressor plugin has this ability, set it to RMS (Root Mean Square) mode. This ensures the compressor reacts to the average volume of the signal over time rather than just the peak value at an instant in time. This is important for buss compression when there are many things going on at once.

BUSS COMPRESSION STEPS

1. Set the *Threshold* at -6dB.

2. Set the *Ratio* to 2:1.

3. Turn *Auto-Gain* off. ALWAYS have auto-gain off. Auto-gain is evil!

4. Play your audio.

5. As audio plays back, keep an eye on the *Gain Reduction* meter and slowly lower the *Threshold* until the loudest sections of your audio make the gain reduction meter read somewhere between -2db and -3dB. No higher.

6. Increase the compressor's *Makeup Gain* by 3dB.

7. Rewind the project and play the track again from the beginning.

8. Take close notice of how it sounds. If anything sounds out of whack, go back and ensure *Auto-Gain* is off and that you're generating no more than 3dB of gain reduction.

BUSS COMPRESSION SUMMARY

If you recall, we reduced the dynamic range of your podcast's vocal tracks by three decibels in the last chapter. Here, we've shaved another two to three decibels off of all sections of the podcast episode. Assuming the mix was good and all sections of the podcast were fairly equal in volume to start with, this additional layer of compression makes the entire episode sound like one smooth, consistent audio program rather than several disconnected pieces stuck together haphazardly.

As with most things in the podcast world, buss compression should be subtle. Not too much. Not too little. Gole-dee-lox.

LIMITING

In the last chapter, we talked briefly about how a limiter is similar to compressor with a very high ratio. In a pinch, you can use a compressor as a limiter. But there are better options for mastering.

In mastering, a limiter has one main goal: Prevent the signal from clipping. Clipping happens when the signal level exceeds 0dB. When this happens, you'll hear a very loud, very uncomfortable clicking noise in your speakers or headphones. It sounds terrible and is difficult to fix. Using a limiter prevents this from happening.

Limiter plugins are usually fairly simple. They typically have the following parameters:

MARGIN (SOMETIMES LABELED CEILING)

This determines the absolute maximum level the audio signal will reach. Some people set this very high – around -0.3dB. Until you've got a little more experience with mastering, I advise starting with a Margin value of -2.0dB.

THRESHOLD

You're familiar with this term from the chapter on compression. In a limiter, the *Threshold* control functions differently. As a refresher, in a Compressor, when you set the threshold, signals above that level are reduced in volume. In a Limiter however, as you lower the *Threshold*, the signal is amplified and pushed upwards toward the *Margin* or *Ceiling* level.

> **Note**: *Instead of a Threshold control, some Limiters will have an Input Gain control. As you increase Input Gain, you amplify the signal toward the Ceiling. In the limiting world, lowering the Threshold and raising the Input Gain produce an identical effect.*

How much limiting is too much? Believe me; you'll know it when you hear it. I like to describe over-limited audio as sounding *crunchy*. Others may refer to it simply as *distorted*. Either way it doesn't sound natural – especially on a vocal recording.

As with Compression, use Limiting very subtly. With a music track containing multiple instruments and a vocal, you can be a little more aggressive. But with a voice-only podcast, I recommend using a Limiter only to keep the one-off signal peaks to -2dB without raising the overall level. If you're certain your episode isn't loud enough and feel the need to boost its overall volume level, slowly lower the Threshold until the Limiter's gain reduction meter reflects a maximum reading of -2dB.

ASSIGNMENT #10

ADD A COMPRESSOR AND LIMITER TO YOUR MASTER BUSS

Today's assignment is to go back to the steps above and configure both a buss compressor and a limiter in your DAW.

Add them one at a time and follow the exact steps outlined in this chapter. At each point, as you play your audio back, turn the compressor on and off, then the limiter on and off.

Each time, take note of the differences in what you hear. If you hear no difference, change the threshold on your compressor or the margin (or ceiling) on your limiter.

Change them until you hear a difference. Go a little overboard. Then back them off until your recording sounds better.

Remember: You'll never get to Carnegie Hall unless you...

Practice.

$[11]$

MP3 Encoding

Note: An early version of this chapter contained step-by-step instructions for configuring iTunes and encoding a WAV file. However, this process is much easier to follow graphically, so I've turned it into an over-the-shoulder video tutorial and added it to this book's companion course. If you haven't already enrolled yet (for free, of course), you can do so at:

http://podcasttechnologycourse.com/intro

IN THIS CHAPTER, we're going to cover the steps required to turn our mastered WAV file into a high-quality MP3 ready for upload to a media host. And for this process, we're going to use a very sophisticated software package known as *iTunes*.

WHY ITUNES?

There are most definitely other options available. But I recommend *iTunes* for four main reasons:

1. *It's free.* As I've mentioned several times already, I advise you to always choose free or close-to-free as long as it doesn't require you to make any big sacrifices in quality, time or energy. Cheap is good. But free is better.

2. *It's available for both Windows and Mac computers* so the process we discuss in this chapter will apply no matter what operating system you're using.

3. *There's a good chance you have it installed on your computer already.* There are so many *iPhones, iPads* and *Apple TVs* in the world, it's highly probable you already have *iTunes* on one of your home computers. If you don't have it installed, I recommend you go to Apple.com, download and install it now so you can follow along with the steps in this chapter.

4. *iTunes uses the Fraunhofer MP3 encoder.* We'll discuss exactly why that's important in the next section.

MP3 CODECs

Note: CODEC is an acronym for "COder / DECoder."

There are two main MP3 CODECs:

1. **LAME** - Stands for **LAME A**in't an **MP3 E**ncoder. (Kind of a *lame* acronym if you ask me.)

2. **Fraunhofer** – Named for the German company that developed it.

LAME is an open source CODEC. You can download it, install it and use it on your computer absolutely free. In fact, if you're using Audacity (the free audio editor we discussed earlier in the book), you have a LAME CODEC at your fingertips.

Fraunhofer, on the other hand, is a commercial product – kind of like Microsoft Office. If you want Excel, Word or Outlook on your computer, you have to pay Microsoft a licensing fee. Same deal with the Fraunhofer CODEC. However, one big difference is that the Fraunhofer license is only available to corporations – not to individuals.

LAME Versus Fraunhofer

If you're encoding music files at high bit-rates – let's say 192 or 320kbps – it's almost impossible to tell the difference in files produced by the LAME and Fraunhofer CODECs. They're pretty much indistinguishable in terms of both quality and size.

But, for encoding spoken word podcasts at lower bit rates, the Fraunhofer CODEC is superior. This opinion is fairly widespread among podcasters and other audio professionals.

> *Note: If you research the LAME vs. Fraunhofer debate on your own, you'll undoubtedly find people who disagree with what I've stated above. I encourage you to perform what's called an ABX test and judge for yourself.*

Fortunately for us, the good people at *Apple Computer* have paid the Fraunhofer licensing fee on our behalf and built it into their *iTunes* software. So, we get to use the best CODEC for podcasters absolutely free. Thank you, *Apple*!

WHY MP3?

Before we go on, let's discuss why we're encoding to MP3 format.

By default, *iTunes* is configured to encode to AAC (*Advanced Audio CODEC*) format. AAC is not a bad format at all. It's a very high quality CODEC and it has good support on Mac and Windows computers and of course on all *Apple*'s iOS devices.

The issue – and this is a big one – is that it's not supported on all devices everywhere. There are still some mobile devices and music players that can't play AAC files. There are even Windows computers without *iTunes* installed that are unable to play AAC files natively without a separate CODEC installation.

By comparison, MP3 has almost global compatibility on all platforms and devices – we're talking 99.9% of all computers, mobile devices and media players on the planet right now. So the bottom line is, encoding your files to MP3 format gives you the greatest possible compatibility with the most devices.

BIT RATES

Let's talk about bit rates for a moment. This topic has the potential to get very technical but we'll keep it at a basic level for the purposes of this discussion.

Bit Rate refers to the number of measurements or snapshots an encoder takes of the audio signal each second. The higher the bit rate, the more measurements the encoder takes. And the more measurements the encoder has, the more closely the output signal will resemble the input signal.

While it's not exactly the same thing, it's helpful to think of bit rates in digital camera terms. Imagine a camera sensor that captures only 1,000 pixels each time the shutter is released. This camera has only 1,000 data points to represent everything in the visual frame. Now imagine a camera sensor with 5 million pixels. Which sensor do you think will capture the clearest image? If printed on 5" x 7" paper, which image will most closely resemble what the eye sees? The answer is easy, right? It's the image created from the camera sensor that recorded the most measurements – the 5M pixel sensor.

In the audio world it's generally the case that an encoder using a higher bit rate will produce a higher quality output file. If bandwidth and storage weren't an issue, we'd all use the highest bit rate available and call it a day.

However, consider that we'll eventually upload our MP3 file to a media host. Consider also that most media hosts charge us per megabyte (MB) of storage. So we have a financial motivation to keep our files reasonably small.

The other thing to consider is that a lot of people who listen to your podcast will download episodes over a cellular connection and larger files eat up bandwidth on their data plans. So, your audience also has a financial interest in your files being small.

All these points considered, when it comes to encoding, we want to find a really good balance between the quality of the file and the size of the file. And if you use the Fraunhofer encoder in *iTunes*, that balance point usually occurs at a bit rate of 64kbps (i.e. 64,000 bits per second) for a mono MP3 file.

MONO VERSUS STEREO

This is a topic we can debate all day. But the reality is that – at the same bit rate – stereo files are twice the size of mono files.

At some point in the future (or now even), you may decide to ignore my advice and encode your files in stereo mode. You may have cool, stereo sound effects or music in your intro. Or maybe you simply enjoy spending money on media hosting. Whatever your motivation, my advice is to be mindful of the points we considered in our discussion on *Bit Rates*. All things being equal, smaller files are preferable to larger files.

Now that we've covered a little theory and rationale, let's discuss the specifics of configuring *iTunes* to produce the highest quality audio while keeping the file size reasonable.

CONFIGURING ITUNES FOR MP3 ENCODING

By default, *iTunes* is configured to encode imported files to AAC format, in stereo mode. As we discussed earlier in the chapter, this configuration isn't ideal for our purposes.

The video tutorial that accompanies this chapter walks through creating a custom *iTunes* import profile with the following features:

1. Stereo Bit Rate: 128 kilobits per second

2. Variable Bit Rate Encoding: Off

3. Sample Rate: 44.100kHz

4. Channels: Mono

5. Smart Encoding Adjustments: Checked (on)

6. Filter Frequencies below 10 Hertz: Checked (on)

ENCODING A WAV FILE TO MP3

Once you've configured *iTunes* according to the parameters outlined above, encoding your mastered podcast WAV file to MP3 is accomplished by following these steps:

1. Drag and drop the WAV file into your *iTunes* Music list.

2. Right-click the file and choose *Create MP3 Version*.

At this point, *iTunes* takes over. The length of time *iTunes* takes to encode your file will depend upon the length of your episode and the speed of your computer. But even a 90-minute WAV file shouldn't take much longer than a minute or two to encode on most modern computers.

The progress bar at the top of the *iTunes* application window will indicate how quickly the encode is progressing. When it's complete, you'll hear a bell. Congratulations! You've just converted your podcast to MP3 format.

ASSIGNMENT #11

CONFIGURE ITUNES AND ENCODE YOUR WAV FILE TO MP3

Follow the steps outlined in this chapter to:

1. Configure *iTunes* for size-to-quality optimized encoding.

2. Convert a mastered WAV file to MP3 format.

[12]

ID3 Tagging

> **Note:** *As with the previous chapter, the process description in this chapter will be very basic. As an owner of this book, a much more detailed, over-the-shoulder demonstration is available in the companion course at:*
>
> *http://podcasttechnologycourse.com/intro*

ONE OF THE INTERESTING THINGS about MP3 files is that – in addition to audio data – they contain embedded information *about* the audio.

This embedded information is how your device (i.e. music player, phone, tablet or computer) is able to magically display the name of the artist and album, release date, album art, etc. on its screen.

For a podcast, this information includes:

- The name of the show

- The name of the host or hosts

- Any show notes you want to include

- The show's artwork – Artwork is important because it's common for listeners to identify with the show's branded image before they identify with its name or (unless you're a celebrity) the name of its host.

All of this information and other key details about how the file should be played is embedded in what are known as *ID3 tags*.

There's no need to get bogged down in the technical details. Just know that *ID3 tags* are where this information is stored inside your podcast's MP3 file.

TAGGING AN MP3 FILE IN ITUNES

The steps required to tag an MP3 file are fairly straightforward.

1. In your Music list, locate your MP3 file, right-click it and choose *Get Info*.

2. In the resulting dialog, select the *Options* tab.

3. Under *media kind*, choose *Podcast*.

4. On this same tab, under *playback*, check both boxes for *Remember playback position* and *Skip when shuffling*.

5. In the same dialog, select the *Details* tab.

6. Under *title*, enter the name of your podcast episode.

7. Under *author*, type your name (or the name of your host.)

8. Under *podcast*, enter the name of your show.

9. *Release date* will default to the current date. You can manually change this if you'd like to.

10. Under *genre*, again choose *Podcast*.

11. Next, select the *Artwork* tab.

12. Drag and drop your show's artwork image into the artwork box.

Note: *From time to time, Apple updates its podcast artwork specifications. To keep up with the latest and greatest, visit Apple's podcasting FAQ at this link:*

http://masterpodcaster.com/itunesfaq

13. Next, select the *Description* tab.

14. Here's where you'll enter your show notes.

Note: *It's a good idea to give some time and attention to your show notes. Make them thorough, compelling and useful to your listeners. Provide HTML links where appropriate. It's also a good idea to write your notes in advance. Assuming you've done that, you can simply copy and paste them into the text box in the iTunes Description tab.*

15. Select the *File* tab. The information on this tab is read only. So you can glance at this page to see details of your file including its size, bit rate, sample rate, etc.

Note: *The most important detail on this tab is the file location. At some point you'll need to navigate to this directory and upload the MP3 file to your media host. Consider copying and pasting the file path to a more convenient location for reference purposes.*

16. When you're done, click *OK*.

The first time I tagged an MP3 in *iTunes*, the file disappeared and I spent several minutes finding it again. Fortunately, you won't have to waste time. Here's the secret:

Once you tag an MP3 file as a Podcast, *iTunes* immediately (and without warning) removes it from your Music library. You can prove this to yourself by scrolling through your music list and searching for it. Or you can trust me and move on.

> **Note:** *Unless you manually delete it, your original, mastered WAV file will remain in your iTunes music library. It should still be in the Unknown Artist / Unknown Album category. Once you locate it, you can confirm it's the WAV file by right-clicking it, choosing Get Info, clicking the File tab and noting the filename has a WAV extension.*

So, where did the MP3 file go? Let's find out.

Go to the *iTunes* toolbar, click the three dots, and choose *Podcasts*. That takes you out of your Music Library and into your Podcast Library.

You'll find all the podcasts to which you've subscribed or have expressed an interest on the left-hand navigation bar. Scroll down until you find your show. Click the artwork, and your show will open in the *iTunes* preview or info pane. Double-click the episode in the info pane to play it. If you hear what you expected to hear, you've found your file.

> **Note:** *It's always a good idea to listen to your encoded podcast prior to uploading it to your media host. This gives you an opportunity to catch any audio glitches or other errors*

before the show is distributed to the masses. Ideally, you'd listen to the show end-to-end at least once before releasing it. If this isn't feasible, I highly recommend you listen to somewhere between six and twelve random sections throughout the length of your episode. Listen for encoding errors, and inconsistencies in volume and overall quality. If you find problems, determine what's causing them and make fixes before releasing the episode.

IMPORTANT NOTE!

If you've followed the steps in this chapter, your show now appears in the *Podcasts* section of your desktop *iTunes* application. However, the episode is only available to *you* on *your* desktop computer. This next sentence is very important.

Your podcast is not yet available for other people to download from the iTunes store.

The good news is, you're 90% of the way there. There are just a few additional steps involved in getting your podcast officially listed in the *iTunes* directory and we'll cover those remaining steps in the next couple of chapters.

ASSIGNMENT #12

USE ITUNES TO TAG YOUR MP3 FILE

Follow the steps outlined in this chapter to add your name, episode description, show notes and artwork to an MP3 file.

[13]

Media Hosting

A S DISCUSSED at the end of the last chapter, the fact that you've successfully encoded and tagged your podcast episode in the *iTunes* desktop application is an important milestone. However, this does not make your show available for others to download from the *iTunes* podcast directory.

The link between your desktop and the *iTunes* directory is your *Media Host.*

More advanced readers may argue, *"You don't need a media host to submit to podcast directories. You only need an RSS feed."* And for the most part, that's true. If you have the time, interest and technical skill, it is in fact possible to become your own media host.

But I can't in good conscience recommend that path to someone who is relatively new to podcasting. There are enough technical hurdles to clear when you're starting out – hosting your own files doesn't need to be one of them. For that reason, I'm not going to cover self-hosting in this book. You'll find plenty of tutorials online if this topic is one you'd like to investigate further.

TODAY'S TOP MEDIA HOSTS

At the moment, there's a fairly small list of what I'll call *serious players* in the podcast media hosting space. A quick Google search will return dozens of names. Regrettably, most of these companies are too small, too new, lack a sound revenue model, or all of the above.

For the purposes of this chapter, we'll focus on only these two top media hosting providers:

- *Libsyn*

- *Blubrry*

> **Note:** *As technology advances and companies flourish and flounder, there's a better than average chance the list of top hosts will change over time. The names on this list are the strongest players in the market at the time this book was published.*

Both *Libsyn* and *Blubrry* have been in business for a number of years, have reliable services, and solid reputations. They've proven they're in podcasting for the long haul. The least expensive hosting plans from either of these companies offer pretty much all the features you'll need when you're starting out. You won't go wrong by doing business with *Libsyn* or *Blubrry*.

KEY MEDIA HOSTING SERVICES

You may be wondering, "*What, exactly does a media host do for me?*" Let's discuss that.

STORAGE

Every podcast listener you ever have will either:

1. Download your episodes to their phone, tablet or computer and play then offline; or

2. Stream your episodes to their device in real time.

Either way, your MP3 files have to be available on the Internet for your listeners to access them. Making these files available for download and streaming is the primary function offered by a media host.

A media host provides an online location to which you upload and store your podcast's MP3 files. The top hosting companies have plenty of storage, fast servers and redundant hardware to protect you from outages and potential data loss.

Most of the top media hosting providers base their pricing on the amount of new storage you require each month. As an example, *Libsyn*'s entry-level 50MB plan allows you to upload close to two hours' worth of podcast content per month – assuming you've encoded your files as recommended in Chapter 11.

Keeping uploaded files available online in subsequent months is built into the host's monthly pricing structure.

DISTRIBUTION

Once your podcast files have a safe place to live, they also need a fast and wide highway over which to travel to your listeners' devices. A good media host will offer high-bandwidth (and often redundant) connections to the Internet so there are no delays when a listener downloads an episode or presses *Play* on their device to stream your show.

RSS FEED

In addition to providing an Internet connection, a media host also handles the technical aspects of wrapping your content in what's known as an RSS feed.

An RSS feed is stream of information in a standardized format that communicates to podcast directories and applications (including *iTunes*, *Stitcher*, *Overcast*, *Downcast* and others) details about your show and each of its episodes.

As you upload new podcast episodes, your media host analyzes them and extracts information embedded in the MP3 files' ID3 tags. The host will often give you an opportunity to manually change the content of the embedded tags if you wish to. The host uses the tag details to construct your RSS feed and ensure it meets the technical requirements of all the podcast directories to which you submit your show.

Best of all, your media host performs all of this tagging and updating behind the scenes. Unless you're curious and want to research it further, you should never *need* to understand any of the technical details of the RSS feed. The only thing you'll ever really *need* to know is where to find your show's RSS URL in your hosts' online interface. You'll need this URL when you submit your show to podcast directories.

STATISTICS

So, your podcast becomes successful. Thousands of people are downloading your episodes every week, and you want to learn more about these mysterious listeners so you can give them more of what they enjoy. Or perhaps you'd like to market a product or service to them. You might even want to attract a sponsor who'll give you a few dollars for every thousand downloads – provided your listeners are in the right demographic.

iTunes can give you this information, right? Wrong.

How about *Stitcher*? Nope.

Spotify? Not gonna happen.

This is where your media host saves the day. Any decent host offers detailed statistics that help answer the following questions:

- How many downloads is my show getting per day (or week, month or year?)

- Which episodes are the most popular?

- What countries do my listeners live in?

- Are more listeners playing the show from their computers or from their mobile devices?

- Are my listeners using Windows or Mac computers?

Answers to some of these questions will be just plain interesting. Others can help you tailor your content, message and approach to the audience members who appreciate it most.

> **Note:** *While I'd never suggest pandering to an audience, giving fans more of what they enjoy is rarely a bad thing. Statistics on the behavior of a large number of listeners provides valuable insight into which of your messages resonates with them.*

Most media hosts will also let you slice and dice this information into pie graphs that show relative percentages and bar charts that allow you to track behavioral changes and identify trends. Some even let you export the data to your desktop so you can manipulate it further in *Microsoft Excel* or *Google Sheets*.

When you're shopping for a media host, pay close attention to the statistics offered with each plan. Sometimes it's worth a small upgrade fee to a plan with better audience insights.

OTHER SERVICES

In addition to the basic features and services we've just discussed, the top-ranked media hosts offer additional services that will undoubtedly be of interest to you now or in the future. This section provides a summary of these services.

CUSTOMER SUPPORT

For even the most technical people, there will be times when you'll need help to resolve an issue that's out of your depth. The better media hosts have support teams that respond to your inquiries quickly and tirelessly until issues are resolved to your satisfaction. You can often get a good idea of how responsive a support team is by sending them a question or two before you subscribe to their service. If their responses are slow or sloppy before you're a customer, that's rarely a good sign.

WEBSITE INTEGRATION

Some hosts offer plugins that allow you to seamlessly integrate your podcast into a WordPress website. The plugin allows you to create show notes, upload your MP3 file, publish the episode to your blog and post to social media all without leaving your own website. This improves the efficiency of your workflow by removing a lot of back and forth between your website and the media host's dashboard.

MIGRATION SUPPORT

If you or your partners host a podcast with *MediaHostA* and want to move it to *MediaHostB*'s platform, it's not uncommon for *MediaHostB* to offer complimentary support to migrate your show's MP3 files, notes and RSS feed to their platform.

If you're brand new to podcasting, you likely won't need this service right now. But it's good to know it's available in case it becomes important to you in the future.

TRAINING

The better hosts offer extensive online training in the form of blog posts, videos, PDFs and webinars to help educate you on the services they offer and how to use them most effectively. Some podcast hosting companies even have their own podcasts about podcasting. Which might sound confusing but really isn't.

SHOW AND EPISODE TAG EDITING

In an earlier chapter, we went into detail on tagging your MP3 files in the desktop *iTunes* application. If that component of your workflow continues to make sense as you gain more experience, there's no reason to change it. However, you should be aware that tagging an MP3 file before you upload it to a media host is usually optional.

The more capable hosts allow you to create tags at the show level – including show name, host name, artwork, etc. – and automatically populate these tags every time you upload a new episode. This has the potential to increase the efficiency of your production workflow.

EPISODE RELEASE SCHEDULING

In exchange for their time and attention, podcast listeners expect a few things. They expect interesting content, solid production quality and consistent release frequency. If you create an expectation with your audience that your weekly show will be available for download at 6:00 AM every Tuesday, each time you fail to meet that expectation, you risk losing listeners.

Whatever podcast frequency you decide upon – daily, weekly, monthly, etc. – there will be times when it's either inconvenient or impossible for you to sit at a computer and click *Publish* at precisely the moment your audience expects your next episode to be available.

Release Scheduling is another killer feature offered by the top media hosts. Assuming your MP3 files are produced, tagged and uploaded to the host's interface in advance, you can set a future release date for each episode. The host keeps your files hidden until the precise date and time you specify. Only then will the episodes be added to your RSS feed, released to the podcast directories and made available for download or streaming. This gives you the flexibility to take a vacation, sleep in, or simply be forgetful and still deliver your podcast content at the exact time your listeners expect it.

CUSTOM MOBILE PLAYER

For an additional fee, some media hosts offer custom mobile apps for your podcast. These apps can be completely customized and branded with your logo, images, fonts and general look-and-feel.

You can provide a custom app to your listeners for free or you can use it to charge listeners for access to your podcast's back catalog.

> **Note**: *Some popular podcasters make 50 or so of their most recent episodes available for free on iTunes and then use a custom mobile app to charge for access to older episodes.*

If you haven't guessed it yet, the custom app is more of an advanced offering. Not only does it cost more for you to support (i.e. by way of monthly hosting fees, as well as fees related to graphic design and any custom development you need) but charging for access to your show is something that most likely won't be profitable until you have a huge following and a large body of work.

My advice is to stick to the basics when you're starting out. You'll have plenty of opportunity to add a custom app in the future if it's something both you and your audience have an interest in.

HOSTING PLAN STORAGE REQUIREMENTS

Most media hosts charge a monthly fee according to the amount of storage space you require. So, as you shop for and compare hosting plans, it's worthwhile to have a general idea what your storage needs will be.

For reference, an MP3 file encoded in mono at 64kbps will contain approximately 28.1MB of data for every hour of encoded content. You can determine your monthly storage requirement using the following formula:

$$[SR] = [Size] \times [Length] \times [Frequency]$$

Where:

[SR] = Storage Requirement

[Size] = 28.1MB per hour (use this as a constant)

[Length] = anticipated length of each podcast episode

[Frequency] = number of episodes per month

EXAMPLE #1

If each episode of your show will be 30 minutes in length and you plan to release four episodes per month, your storage requirement will be:

[SR] = [Size] x [Length] x [Frequency]

[SR] = [28.1MB/hr] x [0.50 hr/episode] x [4 episodes/month]

[SR] = **56.2MB/month**

By this calculation, you'll need a hosting plan that offers at least 56.2MB of monthly storage capacity.

EXAMPLE #2

If instead you want to determine the maximum average episode length you can publish under a 50MB/month storage plan while still releasing four episodes each month, we can calculate that with a little manipulation of the formula above:

[Length] = [SR] / ([Size] x [Frequency])

[Length] = [50MB/mo] / ([28.1MB/hour] x [4 episodes/mo])

[Length] = 0.44484 hours / episode

Converting this to minutes and seconds gives us:

[Length] = **26 minutes and 40 seconds per episode**

SUMMARY

It's important to note that 26 minutes and 40 seconds multiplied by four episodes is a little over 106 minutes. As owner of a 50MB/month hosting plan, you're free to carve up this 106 minutes any way you want. In the extreme case, you could release a single 106-minute episode. The 26 minutes and 40 seconds we've calculated here simply gives you an indication of the average episode duration if your goal was to release four episodes of similar length each month.

In any event, don't worry if you haven't followed the math in this section. These examples are intended only to make you aware there's a fairly straightforward way to calculate storage requirements if you ever need to.

ASSIGNMENT #13

RESEARCH AND CHOOSE A MEDIA HOST

Visit the websites of the following media hosts, review their plans and choose one that meets your needs in terms of features and pricing.

> *Libsyn: http://masterpodcaster.com/libsyn*
>
> *Blubrry: http://masterpodcaster.com/blubrry*

A SPECIAL OFFER FROM LIBSYN

Libsyn is where I've hosted all of my podcasts to date. They're reliable, fast and have great customer service. If you'd like to try them out and get both *the remainder of the current calendar month* and *the entire next calendar month* of hosting for free, use promo code **POWER** when you sign up at this link:

http://masterpodcaster.com/libsyn-promo

[14]

Submitting to iTunes

YOU ARE LIKELY AWARE that *iTunes* isn't the only podcast directory in the world. I highly recommend you submit your show to as many directories as you can – *Stitcher* and *Google Play Music* are two directories worth noting. But recent statistics indicate that somewhere between 70% and 80% of all podcasts are consumed from the *iTunes* directory on iOS devices. That effectively makes *iTunes* the granddaddy of podcast directories. So if you're only able to submit to a single directory, it absolutely, positively must be *iTunes*.

In the balance of this chapter, we'll discuss the steps required to submit your podcast to the *iTunes* directory. As mentioned earlier, don't hesitate to submit to other directories but instructions for doing so won't be covered in this chapter.

LOCATING YOUR RSS FEED URL

Note: Because each media host will provide your iTunes-compatible RSS feed URL in a slightly different location in its online interface, the instructions that follow will be generic. Consult your host's online training and support for specifics.

When you log into your media host, you'll land on some form of default dashboard page that offers an overview of your show, uploaded episodes, summary statistics and other details. From this page, there will be a link labeled *Feed, Destinations* or something similar. On this page, you'll find the URL of your RSS feed.

Note: Typically, an RSS feed URL is of the following format:

http://yourshowslug.mediahostname.com/rss

*If you locate a URL ending in **rss**, there's a good chance that's your RSS feed. If you're still unsure, don't sweat it. In the next section, we're going to confirm you've located the correct URL.*

Using your best judgment, once you've located what you believe is your RSS feed URL, highlight it with your mouse and copy it to your computer's clipboard.

VALIDATING YOUR FEED

In this next step, we'll confirm two important things:

1. Your RSS feed is in fact a valid and *iTunes*-compatible feed.

2. The feed contains all of the necessary metadata (i.e. ID3 tags) *iTunes* requires to make your show available for download from its podcast directory.

Thankfully, both of these are cheap and easy to confirm. We'll use a service called *FeedValidator*.

> ### *FeedValidator:*
>
> *http://feedvalidator.org*

Visit the link above, paste your RSS feed URL into the text box and click the *Validate* button.

FeedValidator will take a second or two to analyze your feed and then provide you with a summary of any problems it finds. If you're using one of the three media hosts recommended in Chapter 13, and you've entered all the important ID3 tags discussed in Chapter 12, any warnings you receive at this point should be very minor and easy to resolve.

If *FeedValidator* indicates you have empty tags, simply return to your media host's dashboard and update them. Then return to *FeedValidator* and click *Validate* once again. Once you no longer receive errors or warnings, you're good to move on.

SUBMITTING YOUR FEED TO ITUNES

It's been a long journey. You've worked hard to record, produce, encode and tag your podcast episodes. You've uploaded them to your media host and you've validated your RSS feed.

Now, it's the moment of truth. The only step remaining is to get your show listed in the *iTunes* directory.

The good news is – the hard work is over. You can practically complete the remaining steps with your eyes closed. But I don't recommend that.

To submit your podcast, we'll use an *Apple* site called *PodcastsConnect*. Here's the link:

Apple PodcastsConnect:

https://podcastsconnect.apple.com

On this page, you'll log in using your *Apple* ID and password – the same ones you use to make purchases on the *iTunes* store. If you don't already have an account, visit the *Apple* ID page at the link below to create one.

Apple ID:

https://appleid.apple.com

Once you've logged in, you'll land on a page titled *My Podcasts*. Assuming you have no other podcasts active in the *iTunes* directory, this screen will be empty except for a blue plus sign in the upper left-hand corner. Click this symbol to add a new podcast.

On the next screen, copy and paste your RSS feed URL into the *URL* field. Before you click submit, give *iTunes* one last chance to validate your feed by clicking *Validate*.

Assuming everything's in order, *PodcastsConnect* will display a Status field next to the URL. A green indicator and a message indicating *Prepared for Submission* means you're good to go.

Below this section you'll find a *Feed Preview* containing your podcast's artwork, description, title, category and related details. At the bottom of the screen, you'll see a list of your available podcast episodes. Review all of this information before you submit. If anything's missing, simply return to your media host and make the necessary corrections.

Once everything looks good, take a deep breath. Click *Submit*. And. That. Is. It!

WHERE'S MY PODCAST?

Apple advises that it can take up to 10 days for your podcast to appear in the *iTunes* store. However, most submissions are approved within three days. When I submitted the *Sure-Fire Podcast*, it was available in the *iTunes* directory within 48 hours.

So, be patient. You may feel compelled to refresh your podcast app every 30 seconds to see if your show is available. Do your best to avoid that temptation. You can thank me later.

Once 48 (or so) hours have passed and your podcast is available...

You've done it.

Congratulations.

You are a Podcaster!

ASSIGNMENT #14

TAKE A WELL-DESERVED BREAK!

Assuming you've followed along with the steps outlined in this chapter, your show is now available in the *iTunes* podcast directory. Start telling your friends, family, co-workers, butcher, baker, candlestick maker – heck, everyone you've ever met – to check out your show.

You've worked hard to reach this point. And now you deserve a break. Take a day or two off. And once you're well rested... start planning your next episode.

[15]

Conclusion

A S I MENTIONED in the preface, there's no way a single book can turn you into an expert podcaster – or an expert *anything* for that matter. As an author, the best I can hope is that you feel more enriched and knowledgeable now than when you started Chapter 1.

I've done my best to provide a solid foundation – to make you aware of and familiar with the tools and techniques you'll need to launch a podcast. But finishing this book marks the start of your journey – not the end. You'll need to combine the information in this book with a fair amount of independent research, practice and patience.

I sincerely hope you've found this book informative and entertaining. But more than that, I hope I've managed to remove some of the mystery, intimidation and overwhelm that technology sometimes creates for non-technical people.

I stated this early in the book but it's worth repeating here:

> *Technology is not the most important aspect of podcasting. But it's extremely important that you understand technology well enough that it doesn't impair the clarity of your message or the quality of your content.*

We're very close to the end of the book. But I hope it's not the end of our relationship. I'm only ever an email away and invite you to contact me with any feedback you'd care to offer on this book or with questions you have about podcasting. You'll find my contact details on the *About the Author* page at the end of the book.

THANK YOU

I want to say a sincere *thank you* for purchasing this book and reading it through to the end. There are dozens of podcasting books available and you chose to spend your time and money on mine. I appreciate that.

If you've found this book valuable, I could use your help. Please visit Amazon and take a moment to leave a fair and honest review of this book. Reviews are the most effective way of letting me know you appreciate the content I'm creating. Your honest feedback will help me continue to create books you'll enjoy reading.

Use the following link to leave an Amazon.com review:

Please leave a review on Amazon.com:

http://davidpower.com/iptreview

Thanks again and best of luck to you.

ABOUT THE AUTHOR

David Power is the host and producer of the *Sure-Fire Podcast* – an audio documentary on the making of an independent feature film called *Sure-Fire*. David's audio recording experience began at the age of 10 – making cassette copies of his parents' Neil Diamond LPs with a handheld microphone. He later went on to acquire a university degree in Electrical Engineering. David now spends much of his time applying the latest and greatest in digital production techniques in both the audio and video domains. He is also an out-of-the-closet lover of Rap music and incorporates dope rhymes into his educational materials at every opportunity. David lives in Brooklyn, New York with his beautiful wife, Cara.

David can be contacted at: david@masterpodcaster.com

Made in the USA
Middletown, DE
17 May 2018